HELPING CUSTOMERS WIN

HELPING CUSTOMERS WIN

CUSTOMER SUCCESS INSIGHTS

PIYUSH AGRAWAL

WINDY CITY
PUBLISHERS

HELPING CUSTOMERS WIN
Customer Success Insights

Windy City Publishers
2118 Plum Grove Road, #349
Rolling Meadows, IL 60008
www.windycitypublishers.com

Published in the United States of America

ISBN:
978-1-941478-97-4

Library of Congress Control Number:
2020907097

Windy City Publishers
Chicago

CONTENTS

PART II
CIRCULAR CUSTOMER TOUCHPOINT PHASES

PART III:
CUSTOMER SUCCESS TEAM AND OPERATIONAL CONSIDERATIONS

INTRODUCTION

WHILE THERE ARE OTHER BOOKS on **customer success**, this book builds on industry standard customer management frameworks, to focus on customer-facing team's soft skills, desired service and business development mindsets, and regular operational considerations to be effective and efficient in these roles. This book is for the savvy business-minded reader who is looking for a real-world solution handbook to use as a practical reference guide throughout their professional career.

I wrote this book for people who work in the information technology industry and who serve customers of software, hardware, and related services. However, many of the ideas and suggestions in this book are equally applicable for customer success managers in other industries and sectors who cater to business customers. Whether you work in information technology or another industry, this book provides valuable insights for anyone dedicated to their customers' success.

Individuals entering the corporate world or looking to navigate up the corporate ladder will find this book useful. Technical resources, transitioning into customer-facing roles, experience the importance of soft skills that were never emphasized in previous positions. Experienced coworkers typically provide on-the-job guidance and the most important lessons to newcomers to be effective in these roles. While technical skills, training, and information can be transferred in much less time, soft skills and corporate etiquette take significant time, since most lessons are learned when related circumstances occur in the workplace. People learn them through hits, misses, sheer embarrassment, and sometimes forced exits over multiple years of their careers. This book lists the skills required to be successful in this role along with numerous examples and suggestions to have a healthy conversation and relationships with customers. It also includes numerous tools, procedures, templates, analysis, and software user experience suggestions to improve customer retention rates.

This book will also benefit management consultants serving the large services sector worldwide. Practicing customer success managers will get an independent perspective to validate or fine-tune their approaches. I include suggestions for supervisors leading customer success organizations to help coach and monitor their customer success managers effectively. This book is also a good general reference on corporate etiquette, which is very important for success in the corporate world. Human resource managers are advised to maintain a copy of this book in their library for newcomers, after validation with the senior staff at their respective organizations.

Readers from startups in Silicon Valley and other centers of innovation worldwide, where focus is predominantly on innovation and customer acquisition, and less on customer success post deployment, will find value in this authoritative guide. The education imparted herewith will help the reader manage the customer relationship through product sale, implementation, deployment, ongoing renewals, upsell and cross-sell opportunities.

Information outlined in this book will help the reader build appealing success stories that will not only help with retention of existing customers but also promote these success stories with prospects. Both marketing and sales departments will benefit from the development of customer success case studies, white papers, e-books, infographics, and blog collateral originating from successful customer engagements.

I have used industry terms common in corporate literature. For instance, the term *vendor* refers to the seller of the product and the employer of the resources serving the customer. References to other terms are also established throughout the book and can be collectively found in the "Glossary" as well.

This book is divided into three parts:

Part I

Customer Success Concepts, introduces the customer success concepts, explains the importance of customer success roles at organizations, and outlines frameworks, metrics, and tools required to set up and monitor progress. It lays the foundation to establish a solid customer success department in your organization and to appreciate Parts II, Circular Customer Touchpoint Phases, and III, Customer Success Team and Operational Considerations, that dive deeper into the numerous lessons I learned while interacting with customers over my multi-decade customer success career.

Part II

Circular Customer Touchpoint Phases, segments touchpoints or interactions with customers in iterative phases: business development and sales, implementation, rollout, adoption, and review. In the sales phase, every customer starts as a prospect whose information and requirements are collected by a company's marketing effort. Subsequently, sales teams get involved to convince the prospect to try to buy vendor's products and services. In the implementation phase, the vendor's implementation team works with customer contacts to give shape to the expectations collected in the sales phase. In the rollout phase—vendor team in collaboration with the customer-assigned champion team—rolls out the software to end users who are provided access to the implemented solution. In the adoption phase, vendor and customer teams continuously check back with the end users to make sure they can make use of the software as intended. In the review and audit phase, vendors and customers independently review progress and achievement of desired milestones. These five phases are iterative, since after the review phase and even through the earlier phases, vendors automatically attempt to enlarge the scope of the sold products and services by urging the customer to buy more and sign up for other projects, which follow the same five-phase approach to realize the proposed value for the customer.

Part III
Customer Success Team and Operational Considerations, covers the softer side of this book. It dives into the key components of a customer success professional's personality, and operational considerations, namely, customer meeting protocols, team setup, management supervision, and operational templates that success professionals can start with or reference for guidance.

Readers can read the book in multiple ways. They can start with the beginning and back sections to get the high-level structure, read the book backwards a few pages, skim the beginning and end sections of each chapter, skim the contents focusing on the call outs, and finally deep dive into relevant stories and experiences based on the emerging interest. Newcomers to the customer success role, or college recruits entering the corporate sector, can read this book start to finish. Existing practitioners can look up chapters or index for specific topics or subtopics. Human resource and senior leadership looking for good training material for their recent recruits, can skim the material, highlight areas for recommendation, or simply strike out content where their perspective differs from what is noted here. Typically, the readers' own experiences will lead them to focus on appropriate sections of the book. After Part I, which is primarily a foundational, industry concept introduction chapter, in Part

II and Part III of the book, readers will find key takeaways at the end of each topic for easy reading and consumption.

Overall, this book will act as a reference as you engage with your customers in this role. Unfortunately, the customer success role is more art than science. The employment of the tactics outlined here will come with practice and experience as you mature in this role.

PART I

CUSTOMER SUCCESS CONCEPTS

The success of any initiative is largely dependent on the quality, discipline, structure, and the mindset of the team running the initiative. I have distilled key elements that underpin an effective customer success program in this part's respective chapters, starting with coverage of important industry terms. To highlight one chapter, "Customer Success Enablers" provides a holistic consideration covering people, process and systems elements. It allows senior executives to ensure all parties working with the customers are hired correctly, trained well and adequately supported by efficient company processes and technology solutions.

This part's contents, as well as the rest of this book, are applicable across industries, customer profiles, and vendor solutions. I have purposefully avoided domain-specific knowledge or guidance. Importance of industry, product, and domain knowledge is a given, well-understood fact and doesn't require further explanation. Most company's training materials cover product or industry-specific information adequately. Contextual knowledge is important to have a meaningful conversation with a customer and to meaningfully implement a solution for any customer.

1

CUSTOMER SUCCESS OVERVIEW

CORPORATE CUSTOMERS LOOKING FOR INFORMATION technology solutions have a lot of options today. Further, even after adopting a software solution for the first one to two years, companies easily switch vendors if the current solution is of subpar quality or value.

Cost of development, selling, implementing, and supporting newer technology solutions has dropped significantly, boosting competition in this space. Amazon, Microsoft, Google, and other data centers worldwide have made it easier for vendors to install their software applications on the **cloud** (i.e. third-party hosting provider infrastructure), avoiding the need to run software on vendor's or customer's hardware. Without the need to buy and maintain expensive hardware, data center infrastructure, heating and cooling systems, this barrier to entry for new competitors no longer exist. Likewise, customers who originally installed software in their own data centers for privacy, security, bandwidth, and other reasons, don't need to use their own data center or resources for any vendor solution, given improved security and privacy risk landscape in the new environment. Accordingly, the migration effort to switch from one vendor to another is much less for the customer, compared to the days in the early 2000s where customers were very protective of their data and installed every software on their own data centers.

Increased competition has resulted in continuous solicitations from vendors that are hungry to uproot existing competitive solutions. Influential customer sponsors, when they move from one employer to another, tend to bring along their favorite vendor solution, putting the existing vendor at a disadvantage. In this environment, the role of the *customer success manager* (CSM) has become very important. The onus to provide quality, consistency, speed, and performance is now entirely on the vendor, under the leadership of the CSM.

The supreme goal of a CSM is to make their customer successful in whatever initiative the customer has set out to do with the CSM's product or solution. It could be for customer's revenue boost, cost reduction, risk mitigation, or a combination of other similar prospective gains.

CSMs are responsible for ensuring that existing customer accounts are not compromised by any potential threat, irrespective of whether it is:

a) **external**—competition, regulatory

b) **customer related**—resource attrition, financial hardship, technology compatibility

c) **CSMs employer related**—product gaps, resource limitations, or general inefficiencies

The customer success manager therefore must be continuously apprised of developments at the customer, in addition to ensuring their software is meeting and exceeding the demands of the customer's end users. Any sloppiness can affect the vendor's (CSM employer) revenue and bottom-line numbers for the year.

HISTORY BEHIND CUSTOMER SUCCESS MANAGER (CSM) ROLE

Formerly, CSMs were called *account managers* and focused on annual maintenance contract renewals. In the early 2000s and before, enterprise software was sold as perpetual software licenses, where 100 percent of the software license was collected in the first year. Ongoing software support, research, and development was offered under annual maintenance contracts to customers for roughly 20 percent of the license cost.

At that time, account managers' key responsibility, from a business development standpoint, was to primarily realize annual maintenance revenue. In such a setup, in most cases the responsibility was on the customer to make the software successful, given that 100 percent of the software costs were already paid in the first year and given that the software was installed in customers' data centers. There were limited refund clauses, in case software didn't turn out to be as successful as promised by the vendor.

In today's cloud-based licensing business environment, roughly a third of the software license is collected in the first year. Further, many customers insist that the license period begins after the software is implemented. The software vendor must not only satisfactorily set up and roll out the implementation at a discounted price, but also ensure that it provides meaningful benefits throughout the life of the implementation. Given this increased responsibility, the vendor contact responsible for customer contact needs to be more mature, skilled, knowledgeable, and generally a senior person from the vendor's organization.

ECONOMICS OF SOFTWARE AS A SERVICE (SAAS) DEPLOYMENTS

The cloud-based vendor solutions explained earlier are popularly sold lately under annual *software as a service* (SaaS) pricing models. The name implies that the software solution is sold as a service to be used for a defined period (as opposed to unlimited timeframe software usage rights sold under the perpetual license models in the 2000s). Pricing is still per licensed user in both cases, unless the vendor offers bulk or enterprise license. The key differentiating point between SaaS and perpetual license is the length of usage per license.

From a profit and loss standpoint, software vendors selling SaaS solutions, make little to no money in the first year, given the very low margin or under-cost implementation fees. Additionally, projects may require rework in the first year on vendors' dime, further negatively affecting breakeven analysis. Vendors make money in the second and third year of the deployments, where support, hosting, and processing costs are minimal, and healthy license fees provide profitable returns.

BOTTOM-LINE VALUE AND COMPENSATION MODEL OF CUSTOMER SUCCESS PROGRAM

Given the SaaS business model explained in the previous section, funding for customer success team headcount and related incentives are tied to the team's impact on a company's reoccurring and incremental revenue drivers as outlined herewith.

Customer Retention

CSMs are expected to maintain or increase customer retention rates through their efforts. Simply put, when a customer drops usage and declines to renew an annual license contract, renewal rate is affected negatively. The higher the renewals, the better for the company, as margins from the second and third year of usage are high. After a few years of a vendor's existence, product quality, nature of the industry, and vendor's research and development investments, determine the percentage of customers that renew year over year. CSMs are incented to exceed this typical percentage, also referred to as a *threshold*, and penalized if unmet.

Key strategic customers should be identified, paid special attention to and retained at any cost. Such customers help with product definition, sales referrals, marketing promotions, and/or provide substantial revenue.

Innovation through constant research and innovation plays an important role in retaining customers, among other factors discussed in this book. Constant provision of newer features with major releases demonstrates continuous investment by the vendor. Customers find this a bonus over and above what they evaluated during the contracting phase.

These investments make the license renewal conversations much easier for the customer success professional.

On a related note, CSMs are incented to pursue multiyear license arrangements to contractually obligate the customer into using the software for more than a year. This reduces reoccurring revenue risk and lowers renewal efforts from both a customer's and vendor's end.

The customer, on the other hand, is very aware of this business model and will agree to multiyear contracts, only if they see value in a vendor's solutions. They will continue to invest in your solution only if they can or are making more money through the vendor's solutions. Strategies and steps outlined in the rest of this book will help you reach these desired contractual arrangements.

Incremental License Revenue

The key difference between hardware and software businesses is the manufacturing or development cost of an additional widget or license. While there is substantial cost to manufacture an additional hardware widget, the cost to offer an added software license on top of an existing software installation is minimal to zero. Software business investors get particularly excited when additional licenses are sold, since the added license revenue almost entirely (subtracting for sales commissions) affects the company's bottom-line. CSMs should constantly be on the lookout to sell additional licenses with minimal extra implementation or installation costs.

With that said, good work cannot be taken for granted. Companies cannot rest on their laurels. They need to continuously deliver additional value over and above previously set expectations. Vendors can do this cost effectively through multiple ways.

Company resources should look for additional uses or applications of the same capabilities. Similar to how a Swiss knife could be used as a knife, scissor, can opener, or screwdriver, a company's product could be used by multiple user profiles for varied tasks. Through ongoing research and conversations with customers, innovative uses can be explored and shared across the customer base. Each of these use cases should be well thought through and supported by working software solutions before they can be shared with customers.

Upsell and Cross-Sell

Upsell and *cross-sell* are almost always used together in sales conversations. Essentially, they respectively refer to selling higher end products and selling other related products to an existing customer. Large software vendors offer a portfolio of software products providing ample options to map vendor's capabilities to customer's multiple needs.

CSMs are urged to form long-lasting customer relationships, so that their customer contacts can share with them emerging opportunities in the customer's environment. I cover responsibilities of senior partners and managing directors of large consulting companies later in this book. CSMs of large software organizations need to have similar skills and personalities. Senior partners at the big four consulting companies walk the halls on customer premises, meeting and greeting new customer contacts on a regular basis. This skill is key to identify upsell and cross-sell opportunities. Once an opportunity is identified, supporting technical staff can map appropriate solutions to customers' emerging needs.

2

CUSTOMER SUCCESS ENABLERS

BUILDING ON MODERN MANAGEMENT CONSULTING frameworks, I have compartmentalized customer success into three interrelated components: people, process, and systems. This framework allows vendors to study, prepare, setup and analyze the effectiveness of each component one at a time, without getting overwhelmed by the enormity of the full customer success initiative. The model comprehensively covers all elements required to make customer success teams successful. While I cover representation from both customer and vendor, the focus is on the vendor to put their best foot forward and address all gaps in these areas. I will touch on a few challenges and mitigating aspects in this short chapter for each area to explain the concept. Readers will find area specific guidance throughout this book.

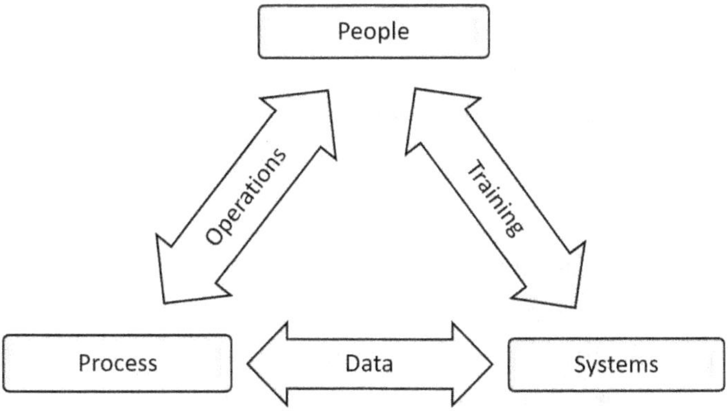

Figure 2.1: Interaction Model – People, Process, and Systems

PEOPLE

A brief definition of all stakeholders involved in buying, selling, implementing, supporting, and using an enterprise solution will help get the perspective of each party that affects the success of any project. The corporate world popularly calls each stakeholder class a persona. CSMs responsibility is to make sure that each persona is engaged, well taken care of, and pleased with the deployed solution. These personas are further explained in Part II, Circular Customer Touchpoint Phases, of this book as they interact with each other during the respective customer touchpoint phases described then. The prefix in the persona title indicates if it represents customer or vendor. Lastly these are the key titles. Based on the customer and vendor's size and complexity, one or more persona could be combined into one or be represented by more than one individual.

Persona Definitions

Customer—Sponsor

Provides funding for the purchased software, service or solution

Customer—Decision Maker

Makes the final purchase decision. Typically, this is a core committee with representation from multiple customer side persona

Customer—Influencer

Performs research on available industry solutions to address a customer need, makes a business case to consider one or more industry offerings, and presents to other customer personae

Customer—Champion

Represents a body of end users with similar needs, defines and articulates requirements, tracks implementation and realization of these requirements, and finally is involved in testing, rollout, training, and ongoing hand holding post deployment

Customer—Project Coordinator / Project Manager

On behalf of customer, manages timecards, project tasks across all customer touchpoint phases (refer to Part II of this book), issue lists, collaboration with all customer personae involved, escalations, execution of customer side tasks, customer side communications and vendor requests for information access

Customer—Solution Administrator

Post deployment, is trained to administer the vendor's product in collaboration with vendor's support team

Customer—End User

Uses the vendor's product after it is fully configured to achieve desired objectives

Customer—Due Diligence Team

Combination of procurement, information technology (IT), and legal group representations, that in collaboration with other customer personae, reviews vendor financial, technical, staffing, security, privacy, administrative, and all other relevant capabilities to continuously enhance and support sold product

Vendor—Sales Executive

Presents the products capabilities, vendor's strengths to convince customer personae to invest in the product

Vendor—Marketing

Through marketing efforts, obtains contacts of customers that are in the market for vendor's products, and sends the information to sales executive for follow-up (a simplified version of the role is provided here, where in reality multiple detailed roles are involved to execute these tasks)

Vendor—Product Marketing

Prepares sales presentation guidelines, brochures, case studies, white papers and other marketing content for generating interest in vendor's products

Vendor—Sales Support

Collects presentation materials and product collateral (brochures, case studies, white papers) from product marketing, and tag teams with sales executives to provide technical information to customers

Vendor—Product Management

Defines and tailors emerging customer needs, makes a business case to enhance product, collaborates with engineering and development teams to develop the enhancement requests, collaborates with marketing and sales to sell the features and provides guidance to implementation and support teams to realize the features for customer needs

Vendor—Project Manager

Executes vendor side project management tasks such as timecards, issue lists, collaboration with all vendor personae involved, escalations, execution of vendor side tasks and vendor side communications

Vendor—Implementation Manager

Configures and implements the solution based on specific customer requirements as gathered from the customer personae outlined above

Vendor—Senior Management

Monitors progress, provides guidance to staff to ensure customers are successful with vendor's products

Vendor—Internal Audit

Audits all or shortlisted implementations using defined checklists and procedures. Documents and presents observations and suggested remediation solutions for projects that are not performing or have not performed well

Vendor—Support Team
Responds to customer queries, logs change requests or issues that limit end users from successfully using the product

Vendor—CSM
Is responsible for defining customer engagement strategy and plan, represents one or more of the vendor personae roles, is involved in all customer touchpoint phases and is accountable for all customer-facing projects. Full set of responsibilities and expectations are outlined throughout this book.

Vendor—Investor
Constantly evaluates vendor financials, retention rates, customer adoption, and success metrics

The quality, availability, attitude, compatibility, and incentives of all involved determine the outcome of any collaborative undertaking. While it is important for senior leadership to be involved for approvals, funding, and supervision, interests of everyone involved must be met. Representative challenges and mitigating factors are outlined in the following table.

People Challenges/CSM Recommendations

CHALLENGE:

Competitive pressures from other vendors limit interest among customers in promoting your solution

RECOMMENDATIONS:

Engage all new management team members

Stay on top of your game and continually engage with all key customers

Don't rest on your laurels; initial project task wins may not be enough for the full project success

Always go beyond talk, and show realized value in every interaction

---

CHALLENGE:

Customer management priorities change, reducing availability of resources and information access

RECOMMENDATION:

For implementations and deployments, plan to do more using vendor's resources with minimal help from customer

---

CHALLENGE:

Insufficient skill set on customer side to adopt solution

RECOMMENDATION:

Plan to adequately train your end users, even at extra non-reimbursed vendor's expense

---

PROCESS

Part II of this book, Circular Customer Touchpoint Phases, outlines the five iterative phases, and related processes, where vendors and customers interact with each other. Suffice to say in this section that the quality of these processes will influence the outcome. Processes should be both designed and executed well. Vendor's senior leadership should have visibility and contribute for the broader customer goals. While metrics for the vendor's product may be realized, if the customer is not able to achieve its larger project goals, such project will still be considered a failure and the vendor may not be able to realize its revenue goals from the engagement.

Borrowing from my previous employer's (a large management consulting firm) engagement model, I propose that every CSM pursue these high-level activities for every customer engagement.

ACTIVITY:
Build Relationship

Description: Using soft skill considerations outlined later in this book, personal charisma, and keen customer service mindset, make lasting friendships with customers. People see through false pretenses so make sure every interaction is genuine and well thought through.

ACTIVITY:
Understand Business Context

Description: Look for the larger project goals in aggregate, customer and third-party resources allocated for the project, integrations with customer's and third-party solutions, level of funding and visibility. This will help in understanding the dependencies, and risks facing the project.

ACTIVITY:
Understand Real Problems

Description: Dig deeper to find out why the customer is investing in your product and other related initiatives. If it is not clear how the project and products under consideration will help resolve customer pain points, ask sooner than later. If a customer's reasoning is flawed, call it out ahead of time, so that realistic expectations can be set, and approaches fine-tuned before the project is undertaken.

You may have noticed that McDonald's installed self-order stations at its locations. What could be the real problems that these stations are trying to address? Is it to minimize the long queues, reduce labor cost for taking customer orders, reduce errors in manually collecting customer orders using service representatives, all the above or something else?

ACTIVITY:
Visualize, Deliver, and Validate Value

Description: Before taking on the project, question the need and applicability of your product. Will it provide value to customer's initiatives? Only when you have a convincing response, bid for the project. After winning the project, follow through to the point value is delivered through your solutions, validated, and acknowledged by all those involved with the project.

ACTIVITY:
Manage Project Plan

Description: Document desired project outcomes, activities, tasks, and milestones to achieve them. Provide continuously visibility and track through completion till value is realized.

ACTIVITY:
Deliver Exceptional Memories

Description: All the previous steps, if executed well, should result in superior customer experience and realization of customer end goals. When customer personnel get rewarded such as with promotions and or higher compensation, due to your efforts, initiatives, intellect, and wisdom, customer delight and gratitude will help you achieve your ongoing revenue goals outlined earlier in this book.

While I talked about the vendor end processes, customer end processes also influence the outcome of a project. Representative process-related challenges and mitigating factors are outlined in the following table.

Process Challenges/CSM Recommendations

CHALLENGE:

Existing customer processes may not work well with your product's capabilities

RECOMMENDATION:

If your product pricing is insignificant compared to the investments the customer has already made in institutionalizing its processes, don't attempt to change existing customer processes to fit your product capabilities

CHALLENGE:

Modifying customer processes may be a time-consuming and expensive undertaking

RECOMMENDATION:

Choose the least resistant approach: Tailor your product to fit the existing customer environment as much as possible

SYSTEMS

The vendor's product itself, along with all supporting technology systems—their access and data—from both vendor and customer end, fall under the systems category. It is important that all supporting systems provide seamless adoption and enabling of the new technology solution to achieve a customer's objectives. Systems underpin the interactions with the other two framework factors: people and processes. See Figure 2.1: Interaction Model—People Process Systems

People should be trained properly on the relevant systems to use them effectively. Systems should be aligned with customers' processes to support on-ground operations—such as manufacturing, people interactions, buying, selling, and distribution. Secured transfer and access to data from operations should be provided to relevant parties.

The key element in all this mix of interacting technology solutions is a vendor's product's user interface. From a conceptual standpoint, I touch on this topic here to explain the interactions between people, process, and systems, and elaborate on detailed consideration such as simplicity and usability in the implementation section of this book.

End users need to use the system for the project to be successful, and accordingly, the product should support end user preferences. While certain end users (typically younger generation users) tend to periodically upgrade and transition to modern interfaces, others don't prefer change. The latter want to locate their information readily using familiar / memorized user views. Product user interfaces should be designed to cater to both categories of end users. "Skin" is a popular term in the software user interface development community and refers to the color, fonts, borders, and other cosmetic elements of a software product's interface. End users should be provided the option to upgrade to newer skins with significant new releases.

Once the product is readily accepted by end users and serves their needs, it will sell on its own. Champion end users will naturally talk about their successes with their colleagues and promote your solution through word of mouth selling.

3

ALIGNMENT WITH CORPORATE BRAND

BRAND DEVELOPMENT IS A GRADUAL effort and takes years to evolve in customer's minds. Unlike consumer product companies' advertising investments in mass media (namely TV and more recently social media forums), business-to-business (B2B) companies pursue targeted marketing and branding efforts via trade shows, industry-specific publications, and social media. I don't elaborate on these marketing channels and urge the reader to access other sources to get a detailed understanding of these channels. Typically, marketing departments are well-versed with this information. If you are curious, there are many good resources, including free online content that you can find via an Internet search. In this chapter, I focus on the content and communication that is projected through these marketing channels. Each of the aspects outlined in this chapter will help you build and support a company's brand or image in the business community. Positive experiences reinforce brand while sub-optimal experiences negatively affect the brand.

PRODUCT MANAGEMENT AND MARKETING

In the early stages of a vendor's formation, it takes a lot of effort and fine-tuning of a product to create a positive experience and desired perception in customers' minds. Over a period, this perception becomes the brand and reputation of the company. Once the perception is validated in a representative focus group, marketing teams align and increase the intensity of their messaging to reinforce this perception. Customer relationship management (CRM) and enterprise resource planning (ERP) vendors, for instance, built their brands over the years using these initial successes.

I use an analogy from a consumer product company to make this point relatable to both technology and non-technology savvy readers. BMW's "driving machine" is a classic brand management example taught in business schools. BMW engineering teams designed their products to create a perception that BMW cars are engineering marvels. BMW cars' handling of user managed controls such as steering wheel, brakes, and accelerators supported the perception of sturdiness and engineering superiority in user's minds. BMW's marketing team then worked alongside the product teams to institutionalize the "driving machine" brand in line with the company's capabilities.

CUSTOMER EXPERIENCE (CX) INTRODUCTION

While customer experience factors matter more for consumer products, its importance shouldn't be minimized for business-to-business transactions. Every company's customer experience and customer success initiatives should be tied to reinforce the desired perception in their customer's and prospect's minds.

Examples

It would be worthwhile to share examples from established organizations that excel in customer experience.

- Amazon's return policy and return avenues (UPS, FedEx, and partner retailers such as Kohl's) provide confidence to shoppers that purchases can be returned easily if the product was ordered in error or is not in line with buyer's expectations.

- Costco's two-year automatic warranty on electronics differentiates itself from other vendors while maintaining competitive pricing. From a personal experience, I was very pleased when Costco sent a technician to repair a $1,600 75-inch TV after it broke down a few months after purchase.

Elements outlined in Part III, "Customer Success Team and Operational Considerations," will help you create the right customer experience when interacting with your customers for business-to-business solutions and products.

Economics

From an economics standpoint, organizations align their customer experience with the price point of the products sold by them:

- Walmart's everyday low-price strategy focuses more on offering lower prices for all its products and less on the look and feel of the customer service area in the store.
- On the other hand, Apple stores have much higher end décor and suave customer representatives given the high price point of Apple phones.

Consistency

Customer experience expectations from a one-time visit at an interstate highway burger joint are markedly different from those providing reoccurring revenue services. While you might excuse sloppy service and a bad tasting experience at a mom-and-pop store that you will likely never visit again, you will not excuse sloppy service from a nationwide burger chain or a high-end corporate service provider. The latter is dependent on ongoing revenue from its customers and needs to provide top-quality, always-available services to its customers while maintaining a superior customer experience. As the scale of the revenue services go up, customers' expectations go up. Service with a smile, by suave, neatly dressed, and articulate customer service professionals are becoming the norm. Customer success professionals are expected to be at their best in front of their customers and behind the scenes to ensure top-quality service provision to their customers.

Periodic Engagement

Balancing a provision of visibility on delivered value while keeping out of the customer's way is an important CSM skill. Customers should never get the impression that the vendor is not around, not available, or not providing value. Through periodic touchpoints such as via quarterly business review (QBR) sessions (which will be explained in Part II, Circular Customer Touchpoint Phases), customers need to be reminded of the value delivered while CSMs proactively collect feedback that may not otherwise be obvious. This approach will streamline the annual license and service renewal conversations immensely.

CX IN CONTEXT OF CUSTOMER SUCCESS

While customer experience seems synonymous with customer success, the latter is the outcome and value that the customer receives from the combination of the vendor's people, process, and systems. Customer experience precedes customer success. Without a good experience the likelihood of the customer's end users using or attempting to use the product will be less. Even if the product works and addresses customer's requirements, inadequately trained/uninformed people and suboptimal processes could prematurely stall the project, affecting renewals and customer retention.

The people process and systems framework outlined earlier explain the factors that influence both customer experience and resulting customer success. Personable, presentable, and sharp resources should be the face of the company. They will lay a strong foundation for ongoing interactions. Subsequently, timely availability of skilled resources will streamline execution of project tasks. Intuitively designed processes—such as contracting, customer support, implementations—will leave a good impression about the company. Lastly, the quality and usability of the sold product and related systems will boost acceptance of the solution enterprise-wide at the customer.

CORPORATE VISION AND MISSION STATEMENTS

Customers and prospects need visibility of the vendor's moral beliefs, larger goals, and targeted space, as encapsulated in corporate vision and mission statements. Vendor resources interacting with external entities should not only know but also truly believe in the vision and mission statements. Customers and prospects see through pretense and lose interest quickly if they don't see this belief in the vendor resources interacting with them. Likewise, corporate vision and mission statements need to be tightly and intuitively aligned with all externally facing vendor collateral, products, and processes.

ADDRESSING BIAS AND PREJUDICE CHALLENGES

Cultural and geopolitical differences can become a hindrance for vendors serving nonlocal markets. These differences could be manifested as deep-rooted prejudices and biases among prospect influencers, decision makers, and sponsors affecting the likelihood of successful business transactions with unfamiliar vendors. In the face of such adversity, vendors can pursue one or more of the following strategies, if feasible, against entrenched competition:

- Cost-effective product development and pricing
- Better quality
- Faster delivery
- Superior customer service
- Targeted marketing
- Diplomatic outreach in case of state affiliated prospects (i.e. government)

After the first few customer successes, perception and brand will establish themselves, making it easier to reinforce and promote the brand throughout this market segment.

REPUTATION MANAGEMENT

Mass media tends to focus on consumer-facing products and services. Reputation loss for a consumer product company can be significant, once mass media picks up and distributes news of compromised safety, hygiene, or quality in a company's products. While business-to-business products and services, which don't directly impact consumer-facing products, aren't covered by mass media, localized media outlets and research analysts covering that space will not hesitate to distribute the news. If not them, competitors will pounce on the news and ensure all customers and prospects receive the news of sloppy product or general customer experience or loss resulting from the transaction. CSMs play a key role in guarding vendor's interests. The customer success framework outlined earlier and all supporting recommendations throughout this book become critically important against this risk.

WORD-OF-MOUTH SELLING

While word-of-mouth selling is prominent in consumer-driven purchases, it is applicable for business transactions as well. Businesses are run by people and people have friends and acquaintances at other businesses. For instance, the auditor community is tightly knit, connected with industry associations such as the powerful association of The Institute of Internal Auditors (IIA). Auditors move from one company to another and spread the message. Superior customer experience and customer success-driven companies maintain an edge over competitors by dominating this selling mechanism.

Research analysts covering the company's market segment also tend to play a role; however, in most cases, coverage by analysts is typically a "pay to play" marketing investment. Smaller vendors that may not be able to afford this investment should instead focus on innovative features in their technology platform. Once these features or products get reasonable momentum in the marketplace, analysts may pick these innovative companies and promote them if their mention is in the best interest of an analyst's research report.

4

SUCCESS MEASUREMENT TOOLS

PROJECT GOALS IN CUSTOMER SUCCESS parlance are also commonly referred to as outcomes or objectives. Irrespectively, they mean the same. Project goals are tied to expectations either preconceived or set by vendor sales teams. For context, sales conversations are largely driven around what exactly customers want and or the possibility of implementing differentiating and innovative solutions that customers haven't thought about yet. Vendor's marketing and sales teams collectively strive to capture customer contacts' imagination and motivate them to make the purchase decision. "Art of the possible," "project vision," and other similar terms are used to achieve this goal leveraging a vendor's capabilities during the courtship period between the vendor and the customer.

To build a sustainable foundation between the two parties, it is important that first vendors only communicate what is possible, well thought through, and tested with vendor's products. Unrealistic ideas will either fall on deaf ears or cause heartburn later during implementations, affecting the relationship irreparably. Second, all portrayed possibilities are captured clearly, realistically, and adequately as project goals with all supporting documentation. CSM's responsibility is to start here and work toward shaping the desired outcomes using the techniques outlined in this book. They need to ensure that this vision or promised outcome is realized during implementations and is monitored post-rollout on an ongoing basis.

The next two sections will focus on measuring progress after the project moves into execution phase and beyond. Collected success metrics outlined here will and should influence CSM team's compensation. Senior level customers (such as sponsors) will accordingly review and compensate performance of the operational customer end personae (such as project coordinators and champions).

CUSTOMER SATISFACTION RATINGS: NET PROMOTER SCORE (NPS) OR EQUIVALENTS

Management terms from the *Harvard Business Review* and other publications have influenced the corporate world's thinking for a long time. Customer satisfaction scores, net promoter scores, and other variations have evolved or morphed into one form or other. As a caretaker of customer success departments, my focus has always been on the objective behind these scores. What actions can I take with this information? Can I prioritize my customer accounts meaningfully so that I can focus my energies on the ones that are most at risk? For the ones that are at risk, is it worth the effort to retain these customers? Are they the right customers given my company's capabilities and the current or expected revenue from the customer? Are the scores a true reflection of my company's capabilities? What is the likelihood that the formula used to calculate the score is accurate and comprehensive enough to provide me the desired information? Am I getting blindsided by using this score? Finally, is it worth the effort to analyze everything quantitatively, when a combination of discrete qualitative groupings combined with descriptive information can do a better job?

My general recommendation is to build customer prioritization models specific for your situation. Templates included in the appendices include several score, filtering, sorting, and grouping categories as examples. You could provide weights to each category and compute aggregate scores if management prefers; however, be aware of the risks as previously outlined. Companies with very large numbers of customers may find it worthwhile to segment their customers using these scores and to distribute the accounts by seniority to customer success staff. Likewise, companies with limited management bandwidth could establish thresholds and escalate attention to senior executives when overall scores deviate from expected norms.

A detailed analysis of net promoter or customer satisfaction scores is outside the scope of this book. However, there are many good resources, including free online content that you can find via an Internet search.

KEY PERFORMANCE INDICATORS (KPI)

Indicators are a potent tool for large organizations to track and manage the health of the company. They are used to prioritize attention, allocate, and compensate resources. Indicators typically fall under two groupings: leading vs. lagging and performance vs. risk indicators. For instance, the increase in the number of users is a performance metric, whereas increase in the number of support cases is a risk metric. Performance metrics reveal improving trends when scores are higher, whereas risk metrics show improving trends when scores go lower.

Indicators are designed to have thresholds, to auto-notify indicator watchers when values go above or below designated thresholds. Customer success software platforms automate this capability, making it easier for company management to watch for trends and be notified when both desired and undesired outcomes occur.

An indicator metric in isolation may not be a good reflection of its intent. Increase in number of support cases could reflect deteriorating quality of software if the number of customers and users are the same. Whereas the same increase in the context of a simultaneous increase in customers and users may not necessarily be a deteriorating condition. A skilled business analyst will be better able to interpret indicator metrics in the larger scheme of events.

Leading indicators forewarn the occurrence of an event before it occurs, and therefore have a predictive element in their definition. As example, a reduced number of weekly user logins over a multi-month period could indicate that the customer is not seeing value in the product implementation and may sooner or later decide not to renew the software license agreement. Lagging indicators, on the other hand, reflect a deteriorating situation explicitly. Dropping revenue numbers of an organization is a lagging indicator and simply conveys the fact that the business is not doing well. Management teams are therefore more interested in leading indicators because they allow them to act before it is too late.

A few of the many indicators that are applicable for customer success departments are:

A) Number of user logins

B) Number of support tickets

C) Periodic usage of product features

D) System response times

E) Number of survey responses

F) Number of positive survey responses

G) Number of contract renewals

H) Number of multi-year renewals

I) Number of open upsell opportunities

J) Number of open cross-sell opportunities

K) Number of realized upsell and likewise cross-sell deals

L) Revenue increase

M) Cost reduction

N) Time to implement product

O) Time to onboard users

P) Escalations to management across customers

RED FLAGS

In addition to the quantitative factors represented by customer satisfaction, NPS, and indicator metrics, qualitative information is equally important, if not more so, to ensure continued success of the customer in context of a company's products and continued revenue stream. Customer success professionals are advised to watch for negative indicators, or red flags, such as attrition of customer resources involved with the project, ongoing budget allocation pertaining to the vendor's product, customer's financial health, reputation, or other significant risks applicable to the customer's industry. Each one of these risks can have a potent impact on the health of the project. Customer-facing resources such as customer support, implementation, and sales teams should always be on the lookout for such developments in every interaction with the customer. Vendors should provide appropriate forums to disseminate this information across all customer-facing resources.

5

DRIVING EFFICIENCY

INTERACTING AND COLLABORATING WITH CUSTOMERS can take a significant toll on the CSM's effectiveness, as well as work-life balance. Arranging meetings, planning, collecting data, preparing, executing, handling customer complaints and escalations can be a challenge. Effectiveness and efficiency in the execution of these tasks can minimize both customer's and customer success manager's time and improve the customer experience factor as well. Ideas shared in this chapter will help managers do more with less.

KNOWLEDGE REPOSITORY

Big four consulting companies historically took the lead in establishing knowledge repositories for internal use first and then to share information and training selectively with external parties. The knowledge repository concept has caught on and is pursued by most large vendors now. It allows sharing among colleagues of best practices and lessons learned by senior vendor personnel. Customers appreciate this emerging, constantly updated stream of information, and expect their vendor contacts to share relevant information timely and contextually.

Vendors should disseminate this information with care. As lessons are learned, relevant vendor resources should publish this information on knowledge-sharing forums, discuss with peers to agree on a consistent external communication update, then train all relevant staff to use this formalized information for communicating with clients. Establishing and driving a consistent message outside the organization is important for minimizing confusion among both internal and external audiences.

Knowledge repositories are also a good place to host technical and business development training materials. Questions and topics such as "how are the vendor's products useful for customers' needs," "how is the vendor product configured and implemented," "what messaging should I use to engage with prospects," should be answerable with the training content in these repositories. New recruits will find this business and technical knowledge useful in interacting with customers.

CUSTOMER SUCCESS TECHNOLOGY SOLUTION

A technology platform underpins a significant part of the efficiency and effectiveness playbook, drawing from American football terminology. It helps automate, driving a consistent experience and success approach among all CSM professionals at a given vendor. (Complete value proposition of such solutions can be obtained from technology providers' websites. I cover only the salient points in context of the messages outlined in this book.) Key performance and risk indicators, customer satisfaction scores, product goals, action items, assigned customer and vendor resource details, notifications, collaterals, feedback tools and surveys, dashboards, reporting, analysis, and integration with third-party systems, collectively become a monumental undertaking that can only be managed through a technology platform for large vendors. Sharing guidance and collaboration become much easier with such a solution.

Providing information as and when needed also helps engage the customer. Given the challenges inherent with cloud-based solutions outlined in previous chapters, out of sight, out of mind is a significant risk and shouldn't be taken lightly. Customers should constantly be apprised of the value provided by a vendor's solutions. A technology-based solution cost effectively provides continuous visibility and always keeps the vendor's brand at the forefront.

Customers should be encouraged to bookmark the link to the platform to access implementation notes, training materials, corporate documentation such as product vision and roadmap, company updates, business development presentations, and product brochures. Even if other solutions exist that house this documentation, it is okay to provide redundancy. Duplication will not hurt if the information is kept updated. From my standpoint, a customer success technology platform is the ideal location for customers to access such vendor information.

This technology solution can also be used to insert meaningful updates to the customer's daily communication platforms such as email, corporate chat, and mobile interfaces. In addition to project specific updates, daily or periodic tips and tricks techniques can be pursued to stay uppermost in the customer's mind.

CUSTOMER SUCCESS DEPARTMENT MATURITY MODEL

Taking a leaf from one of the established software maturity model frameworks from the industry, customer success framework at a given organization can be rated using Carnegie Mellon's Capability Maturity Model (CMM). While actual definitions are not important, key considerations outlined here will help company's customer success teams mature with periodic investments in people, processes, and systems.

Carnegie Mellon's Capability Maturity model has 5 levels that I outline in this section. I have repurposed these levels to outline the state of each level and key considerations required to move up the maturity curve, in context of the customer success capabilities of a vendor organization. This characterization is by no means a formal accreditation framework and serves only to guide any vendor to get better in executing its customer success responsibilities. The maturity levels are distinguished by the following characteristics:

1. Initial
2. Repeatable
3. Defined
4. Managed
5. Optimizing

Level 1—*Initial (Undocumented, Reactive, and Ad hoc)*

Customer success setup is not well-defined or organized. Dedicated customer success resources are not allocated to customers. Company resources from other departments such as implementation, product management, sales support, or marketing are requested to manage customer relationships when the situation has already aggravated. There is no reference documentation on the process, customer accounts, and historic interactions with customers.

Minimal success is dependent on a few skilled and passionate company employees who keep the customer relationships afloat with part-time responsibilities. New employees find it difficult to onboard themselves and require extensive shadowing with senior colleagues.

Level 2—*Repeatable*

Skilled customer success resources take the initiative to document a few key success stories and supporting process documentation such as typical implementation steps, customer success metrics, root causes, and remediation efforts. Key company personnel interacting with customers are tasked with consistent execution of these processes. However, adequate monitoring of process execution is not undertaken due to limited management bandwidth.

Level 3—*Defined*

Experienced resources define and document all processes relevant for interacting with customers. Expected outcomes and success metrics as defined in this book are documented. Metrics are expected to be collected, analyzed, and shared for instance, among other customer success process expectations as previously outlined. All relevant customer interaction resources are required to follow these set processes. However, with not enough customer success examples to build on and validate, the processes are not fully tested and validated for enough future customer implementation possibilities. Inexperienced resources need to reach out to senior colleagues for impromptu guidance in unanticipated situations.

Level 4—*Managed (Capable)*

Consistently collected process metrics validate effective achievement of desired outcomes across a wide range of customer profiles and implementation setups. A company has invested in audit and quality management resources to test defined and documented processes across a wide variety of conditions. Processes are found to be competent and have variability by design to adapt dynamically in environment variations without compromising quality.

To achieve this level, companies must have implemented their solution successfully at numerous customer accounts under varying customer circumstances. For example, the product is implemented at customers representing numerous industries—such as retail, finance and manufacturing—for a range of users. The data set representing these implementations could also vary from a small to extremely large databases. The number of metrics and their relationships to each other for consideration could likewise vary from a handful to a sizeable number. A few examples of these metrics could include the number of users, their login frequency, impact to customer's revenue or cost figures, leading and lagging indicators that collectively or individually predict customer success.

Level 5—*Optimizing (Efficient)*

With the previous maturity levels under the company's belt, companies focus on constantly evaluating and executing process improvement opportunities without adversely affecting desired outcomes. The goal is to constantly enhance the customer delight factor with cost-effective investments in people, process, and systems factors. Better team alignment, more skilled resources, dedicated personnel, clearer and visually appealing documentation, and better technology systems are just a few of the many opportunities that companies can invest in to continuously optimize their customer success capabilities.

PART II

CIRCULAR CUSTOMER TOUCHPOINT PHASES

In this part, I will dive deeper into all the phases where vendors interact with customers. These phases are circular since, after every cycle, there is an opportunity to sell more services and products and to repeat the process. As outlined in "Bottom-line Value and Compensation Model of Customer Success Program" section of Chapter 1, CSMs are incented and should be motivated to keep repeating this cycle to boost vendor revenue. Excellence in each phase will be a strong foundation for the next phase and the next cycle iteration. I recommend readers look back at the "People" section under Chapter 2 titled "Customer Success Enablers" to understand the actors involved in each of these phases. Before a company becomes a paying customer, it is a prospect. Customers are interchangeably referenced as prospects in this phase.

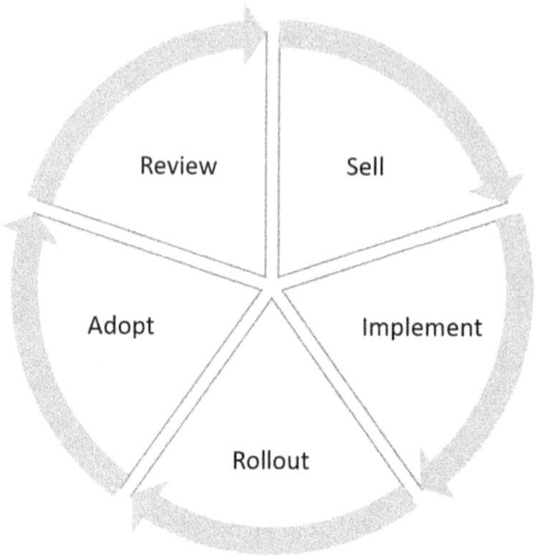

Figure II.1: Customer Success Touchpoint Cycle

6

SELL: BUSINESS DEVELOPMENT AND SALES

CUSTOMER SUCCESS INTERACTION STARTS FROM the sales phase and to some extent marketing, through which vendors attempt to obtain contacts of prospect companies possibly interested in vendor products and services. Each interaction—from discovery, product demonstration, proposal development, and contracting—is an opportunity to impress the customer and provide a superior customer experience. In this phase, from the customer success standpoint—expected outcomes—key performance metrics are documented clearly in a customer success solution and shared with the customer contacts, sponsors, influencers, and decision makers. With clear expectations and supported documentation, software implementation, rollout, adoption, and ongoing renewals become much easier undertakings.

While the sales executive is on point to convert the lead into an account, the CSM is responsible for ensuring that the customer achieves their goals after the contract is signed and should accordingly work on the foundational elements outlined in Part I, Customer Success Concepts, in this sales phase. These include documentation of outcomes, success metrics, and capturing customer details. While every vendor will have varying management hierarchies, I suggest that the assigned CSM is on point for all post-sales phases activities while staying in the loop during the sales phase. Customer experience and success responsibilities in the sales phase should be jointly handled by sales and marketing teams.

Typical Sales Process

While limited smooth talker sales personnel can get away with selling unneeded products, most enterprise investments are need based. Typically, customer end users express a need for a solution to their management, who then appoints a champion to represent the end user's interests. The champion collaborates with the influencer to analyze detailed requirements, options available in the market, pricing, time frames, expected value, and return on investment. The influencer prepares and makes a business case for a solution to sponsor. The latter reviews the budget for this year and next, makes funding arrangements, and identifies a project manager to coordinate the rest of the purchasing process. The latter invites vendors to bid for work, and coordinates in shortlisting and final selection in collaboration with all customer end roles (refer to the full list in the "People" section of Chapter 2). Diligence persona looks at relevant vendor financial, technical, usability, staffing, security, privacy, administrative, and all other relevant capabilities before sales contracts are finalized.

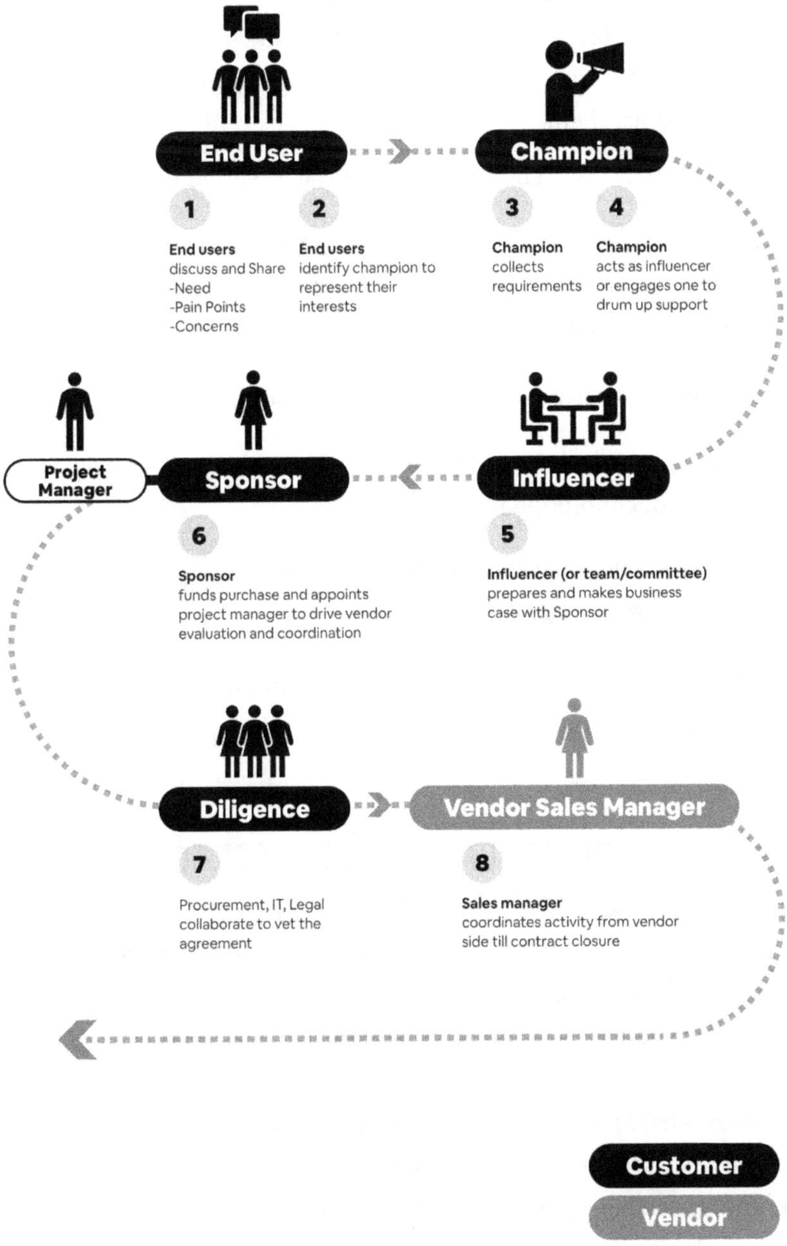

Figure 6.1: Typical Sales Process

Challenges Relevant for CSMs in This Phase

The following are few challenges common at organizations. Chapter 5, titled "Driving Efficiency" provides several mitigating solutions to prepare and protect against them.

1. Project objectives siloed in contract statements and proposals
2. Competing priorities between customers at time of project execution, to the point that formerly set goals are neither aired in later phases nor realized
3. Customer information not documented and retained
4. Customer side responsibilities reassigned during the five customer touchpoint phases
5. Key and influential customer contacts' interest in project diluted and priorities changed
6. Renewals, cross-sell and upsell opportunities compromised, making the project unprofitable for vendor

QUALITY OF COLLATERALS AND TALK TRACKS

The term "talk tracks" refers to the verbiage used by sales teams to make the sale. This includes information such as "why is the vendor's product better than others," "capabilities of the product," and "vendor's strengths on top of its product-based capabilities." Standardized sales and marketing talk tracks and collaterals are typically created by product marketers in collaboration with sales, product, and engineering leadership of vendor organizations. Prospect-specific content is prepared by sales engineers or sales staff under the leadership of the sales leader assigned to the account.

During this phase, very limited time is available from customers. Sensing time constraints, novice vendors tend to convey a lot of information in less time. On the contrary, talk and show less, to the point and with quality words and visuals. Follow a customer's lead, let them talk more, and respond when requested. Listen to their requirements carefully. Customers are interested in all relevant vendor details, and if they are interested, they will reach out.

There is an information sharing balance that needs to be pursued in this phase. Share enough to keep them interested and motivated until the contract is signed. During sales conversations, it is better to not expose everything. Have them ask for more. Keep them engaged as they make a business case internally, get funds, and complete the vendor evaluation process. Leave open the possibility of sharing data gradually by providing a pretext to reach out and ask for status. Additionally, always be mindful of not revealing competitive information that could be used against you and in favor of competition during sales conversations. While vendors do require signed non-disclosure agreements (NDAs), it is not much of a deterrence in practice.

Whatever you say should be well thought through. Presentations, notes, contracts, and proposals should be of top-notch quality. Both aesthetics and content of the shared materials should be appealing and compelling. Engage a designer to ensure that the materials are pleasing to the eye and intellectually excite customers' minds at the same time. As a rule, your information will be reviewed with interest if it is pleasing to the eye first. Readers tend to glance and skim through sales and marketing literature before they deep dive further for detailed information. If the visuals are not attractive, you will lose the opportunity to get the first favorable impression.

Make it easy for the customer to grasp the message. People always have too much to read. Start with a summary, get to the point, and then lead the reader through detail. Good readers scan every document, front and back, looking for the key point. Once they locate it, they zero in. If they cannot find the summary fast, they will reject, move on, or deprioritize your project. For reference literature, refer to publicly available marketing materials from large information technology software and services companies.

KEY TAKEAWAYS

Talk less and with quality

Ensure collaterals are pleasing to the eye and appeal to customers' minds at the same time

HELP PROSPECTS MAKE A BUSINESS CASE FOR YOUR SOLUTION

Give your prospects the time and resources to make your solution's business case to their executives. Proactively think and provide materials that will make it easier for the prospect contact to consume and use for their own presentations to senior executives. Use the business case argument to have them create a budget for your product if not obtained already. Tapping into money left over from some other product's budget is another possibility. All this potential effort from prospects is conditional on potential buyers' and sponsors' belief in your product's value proposition.

Structure pricing so that it is simple to understand, is flexible, with tiered options, and is in line with customer budget. Simplicity minimizes conflicts and misunderstanding during contract negotiations, implementation, and renewals. Always propose the least resistance approach and ensure pricing consistency across all customers. This will also drive consistency across your sales and marketing collaterals, making the lives of all your customer-facing resources easier.

Product pricing decisions are handled by senior vendor leadership. The previous recommendations are more for them than for the CSM. CSM group leadership should have influence on pricing models and take appropriate feedback from on the ground CSM staff interacting with customers on a regular basis. As a quick primer, pricing is influenced by product cost, company overhead, competitive pressures, and price sensitivity of customer.

KEY TAKEAWAYS

Offer simple to understand and flexible pricing terms

Check for budget, make a business case to create budget, and stay within budget

CHOOSE YOUR CUSTOMERS

Sales, marketing, and CSM staff should have a clear understanding of their own products, business models, and targeted customer profile. While this consideration is more applicable for vendor's senior management, related inefficiencies and inconsistences can have significant revenue and cost impact and setup the CSM for failure in the next four phases.

For instance, never use a direct sales force to sell to low budget/low volume accounts. Numerous startups fall into this trap, thinking that it is easier to get small customers before selling to large ones. When they do manage at times to get into the large accounts, the effort required to service the small existing accounts remains substantial and drains company resources. The key is to refine the business model and identify your sweet spot fast. If you are starting a new business model fail fast, refine, test, and scale.

If the low budget/low volume accounts are not your sweet spot, politely decline to pursue this segment, deprioritize existing, and move on. Likewise, if you serve a mass market customer base with a very low touch service and support model, decline to serve large accounts that require dedicated service and support teams.

One of the CEOs I worked with famously said "certain prospects are better off with my competitors." He is right. Get a sense of the demands placed by your prospects during negotiations and weigh those demands against the potential to grow revenue.

Many times, products that don't make sense are sold to customers to make up for sales targets. High-level customer executives could get influenced into signing deals, leveraging corporate relationships, or common investors. But, after the sale, it becomes an uphill battle to implement the solution and to adopt it, if people on the ground don't appreciate and find value in the solution.

Despite limited alignment of vendor's product with prospects' needs, vendor sales executives persistently knock on prospects' doors, work the phone lines, emails, and other desperate measures, not realizing that they can push the needle only so far. Building on the square peg in a round hole analogy, if something is not meant to be, it is not meant to be. Executive influence can only go so far. Effort from both vendor and customer sides may not be worth it given these situations. For senior vendor executives it can be difficult to bite this bullet and accept this reality. I recommend that they do, sooner than later.

KEY TAKEAWAYS

Low paying and high maintenance customers are not worth their name if you are not able to leverage those relationships for selling into new accounts

While it is worthwhile to engage them early on in your business lifecycle to test product concept, cost considerations should deprioritize effort to maintain their implementations

DON'T BURN BRIDGES

Mid-size to large consulting companies offer numerous service offerings and look for repeat business from customers. They assign senior staff to accounts for periodic follow-ups. Winning and losing request for proposals

(RFPs) to other consulting vendors doesn't mean an end to these relationships, since other opportunities are sometimes in the pipeline at the same customer. Do not close the door because you may have other possibilities now or in the future.

Additionally, customer service is in a consulting company's DNA. For context, senior-most staff—popularly called company partner, managing director, executive director or equivalent—treasure their assigned accounts. Each senior assigned resource is responsible for nurturing their accounts, selling the full portfolio of services offered by the consulting organization. As account owner, their focus is customer satisfaction. Depending on the scale and extent of the damage to the account, any misstep by anyone under the senior resource serving the account, could result in cause for termination of both the senior person and the person causing the misstep.

On the other hand, smaller software companies and startups are typically into one trick pony software sales. When their solution loses out to competitors' solution, such companies think that the relationship is lost. One sales manager I know came out hard on the prospect contact after he lost the RFP. The prospect contact, who was formerly part of the salesperson's Rolodex, shared the futility of this outburst with me after the incident.

Software vendors, with such limited offerings, participate in few RFPs and attempt to stay in the account through the stickiness of their software implementation. I covered in Part I, Customer Success Concepts, how no software implementation is permanent at any company for a given domain area. There is always room for competitors to get into the account after losing the RFP during a formal evaluation process. Most large customers engage more than one vendor and maintain more than one implementation as a backup solution. Given the churn, company closures, and merger and acquisition activity in the software industry, there is always a possibility that another bid will open in the future and the rejected vendor is invited again. Customers realize that innovation is constantly happening, so a deprioritized vendor may become a force to reckon with in the future.

Software companies, big and small, need to take a lesson from consulting companies' mindset and treasure each prospect relationship even if it doesn't turn into a business transaction in the first few rounds of conversations.

KEY TAKEAWAY

Maintain contact with prospects that didn't select your software in the first round

ALLIANCES BETWEEN SOFTWARE AND SERVICES PARTNERS

Out of sight/out of mind is a human psychological trait that causes failed deployments after the implementation team is out of the picture. To address this, large software vendors explore mutually beneficial partnership arrangements with consulting companies that are present onsite for long durations.

Internal audit projects, or ongoing IT hardware/network support projects, for example, tend to be multi-year relationships. Alliance with such consulting partners can make the onsite partner your local champion, vouching for your interest during their periodic interaction with customer contacts. In return, software vendors offer service opportunities related to their software implementations to their partners and invest in training partners' services personnel.

KEY TAKEAWAYS

Build alliances with services organizations that are engaged in long duration projects with the customer

With proper incentives they will vouch for your interests in your absence

EXPLORING UPSELL AND CROSS-SELL OPPORTUNITIES

Coming back to the circular nature of the five phases, once a product or solution is successfully implemented for a customer, CSMs in collaboration with sales executives or themselves, based on vendor's incentive model, should begin to look for upsell and cross-sell opportunities. While this topic is covered in the section titled "Bottom-line Value and Compensation Model of Customer Success Program" in Chapter 1, I touch on behavioral nuances here during such conversations.

After deployment, software companies pursue periodic business or adoption reviews, also called quarterly business reviews (QBRs), with the customer. Vendors don't have to stick with quarterly schedules and can vary the frequency based on the situation. This topic is addressed at length in Chapter 9 titled "Adopt." Such meetings are ideal for bringing up other potential and meaningful opportunities if the previous product or service deployment is a success.

Customers, while open to hearing about other opportunities, don't appreciate aggressive selling during such adoption or business review sessions. A subtle, consultative approach works best in such situations. Whether you are selling, implementing, or following up on adoptions, always go with some different nuance, or nugget of information to your customer. You will create an image of a resourceful contact among your customer base and will always feel welcome whenever you reach out to them. Don't expose the full bag of information in one meeting. Gradually trickle through this information so that you stay engaged and have a reason to go to the customer exploring business development opportunities every now and then.

KEY TAKEAWAYS

People like to buy from and work with people they like or are impressed by

Offer meaningful business value and your customer contacts will not hesitate to invest further in your relationship with them

7

IMPLEMENT

THE CSM ROLE BECOMES PROMINENT starting with the implementation phase. Depending on the resource allocation and size of the vendor, the CSM role can be technical, and can act as implementation manager and product manager as well. Alternately, CSM could simply play a supervisory role, akin to the senior-most staff at large consulting organizations, as described in the previous chapter in the "Don't Burn Bridges" section.

Building on the outcome concept, clearly defined and realistic goals are key to the success of any project. All parties involved need to document desired outcomes based on the resources, time constraints, skills, and capabilities of the people, process, and systems under consideration, tying back to the customer success framework from Part I of this book. Simplicity in documentation, talk track, negotiations, requirements, and project planning will provide clarity to everyone involved.

Parties involved need to negotiate what is possible given constraints, and then build project plans keeping this desired end in mind. Once the execution framework is in place, project managers from all parties need to continuously monitor and course correct knowing fully well that certain objectives may need adjustment as more visibility is attained during project execution. This flexibility is important and should be expected from project sponsors. Reasonable and mature executives understand this expectation and are willing to reorient project requirements if alternatives are thought through and understandable justifications are conveyed to executives.

Continuously updated documentation with audit trails will set up projects for success. In the worst case, if projects fail under the worst unanticipated conditions, or when circumstances are beyond the involved team's control, this audit trail will save ground level resources and supervising executives from tough postmortem analysis of failed projects.

Success and failures are part of a mixed bag. Failures can be avoided, but when people attempt to chart uncharted territories, unexpected circumstances do occur. In this situation, it is important to stand up again, learn, course correct, and keep going. Success is built on failures, brick by brick and in the case of customer success function, one customer at a time. The entire organization should support the customer success function during adversities. Lessons learned from both successful and unsuccessful deployments will pave the way for the next successful one.

Most vendors have a good handle on their respective implementation processes. Accordingly, the contents documented for this phase are designed to simply provide an overview of a typical implementation model, while focusing primarily on overcoming challenges experienced during execution.

Typical Implementation Process

Outcomes need to be supported by detailed requirements and business analysis. Information collected during the sales phase should be transferred to the vendor resources involved in the implementation phase. Customer influencers, champions, sponsors, and project coordinators, except for the due diligence team, are required to stay engaged with the implementation phases and beyond to establish this continuity. This customer group is explicitly called out in most vendors' implementation frameworks and is provided vendor specific names for reference, such as Tiger team. The actual name doesn't matter. I will use this name to reference this customer group in this book. Tiger team establishes a reporting hierarchy among themselves to collaborate with the vendor resources and to communicate within the group. It works with the vendor to transfer requirement details, clarifications as and when requested by the vendor. Vendor's sales team accordingly transfers information they collected during the sales phase. Best practices communicated in Part I of this book, such as use of a customer management solution, documentation, and visibility of customer expectations, should be adhered to make the process seamless and to ensure that nothing falls through the cracks.

A vendor's implementation manager and customer project coordinator collaborate to distill requirements into actionable tasks and communicate the resulting project plan to all stakeholders involved. Vendor's senior management and customer sponsor review plans, monitor progress, and provide guidance to respective sides. Escalations between customer and vendor is handled by this senior staff. For training-related activities, vendors first train representatives of the Tiger team to validate solutions, its value, and prepared training materials. Tiger team representatives are typically on point to train the rest of the end user community. I recommend that the vendor stays involved in training as many users as it can while maintaining professional services costs.

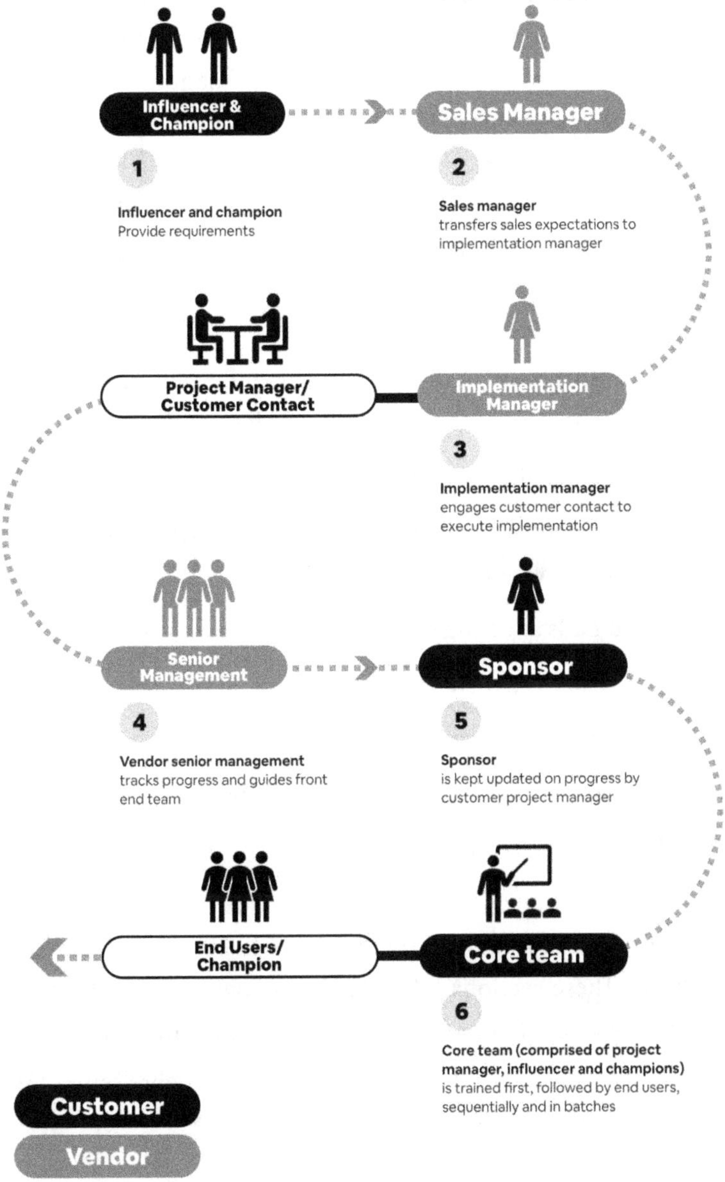

Figure 7.1: Typical Implementation Process

High-Level Implementation Challenges

I touch on a few challenges here to lay the groundwork for the rest of the chapter. Implementation phase requires a combination of technical and, most importantly, soft skills to be effective. Challenges outlined below can be overwhelming for technical staff and should be handled by senior CSM resources. Guidance provided in the rest of this chapter will help you think through and prepare situation-specific remedies for these and other challenges outlined herewith.

1. Potential change of guard on customer end resulting in motivation challenges, failure to proceed, and lack of timely responses
2. Changed or unclear requirements
3. Personal chemistry issues or cultural differences between customer and vendor contact
4. Dropped balls affecting credibility
5. Lack of visibility for stakeholders
6. Usability issues, missed requirements, delays
7. Coordination, accountability, team turnover
8. Inadequate notes causing communication gaps

For easy understanding, I divide the rest of the topics in this phase into three sections. These sections follow a chronological order. While Figure 7.1 conveys the sequential nature of high-level implementation activities, the softer, i.e. soft skill considerations, required to be successful in this job are best compartmentalized in these three groupings.

- Team Introductions and Preparation
- Planning
- Execution

TEAM INTRODUCTIONS AND PREPARATIONS

This section will help the assigned vendor implementation team create the best first impression with their customer counterparts. It covers guidance for buyer inertia, vendor/customer team bonding, team set up and high-level protocols to get on the right side of all influential team members. I cover team and operational considerations more thoroughly in Part III, Customer Success Team and Operational Considerations.

Implementation Team Setup

Most vendors know how to staff their projects from their own end. They also prepare and publish a good list of participation roles from customer side too.

For reference, depending on the scale of the project, vendor side participation may include a vice president, consulting partner, architect, project manager, or technology resources both onsite and offsite. Customer side participation may include a corresponding project manager, champion end users, project sponsor, a team of supporting domain experts, infrastructure security resources and more.

While it may sound obvious, I recommend that projects be staffed well, even under cost constraints. Project governance or team setup gaps on either side—vendor or customer—can make or break projects. High priority projects should receive appropriate attention from key company leaders from both vendor and customer end. In addition to project staffing, access to data and supporting systems should be authorized and supported by the right individuals from both organizations.

Customer organizations have competing priorities and fight political battles internally to access the meager resources required to complete existing projects. Nice to have solutions typically get scant or minimal attention. "Nice to have" is a term used for non-crucial solutions or features. Such solutions, even if agreed and contracted with effective sales tactics, are always pushed to the end and hard to get off the ground.

KEY TAKEAWAYS

Project governance is important

Nice-to-have projects will always receive scant attention

Vendor will need to leverage superior customer success skills to rise in priority

Customer Motivation

Handling customer interactions can be a very frustrating experience. Lack of timely response, misunderstandings, and slow pace can enervate the most enthusiastic and experienced customer success managers. Partial attentiveness, by customer contacts, to vendor requests, failed configurations undertaken by inexperienced customer staff, reassignment of project staff, and project sponsor exit can result in rework and or project delays.

If the customer is motivated and is collaborating proactively, the rest of this section may not apply. If not, then there are ways to remediate this situation.

Customer contacts typically have numerous tasks on their plate, each seemingly more important than the other. Daily prioritization is always a struggle. It becomes the responsibility of the customer success lead to raise his or her project's priority in customer's mind set. Most naïve resources or newcomers to this role resort to excessive emailing, calls, or requests for onsite visits, which tend to have an opposite effect and end up annoying the customer.

A more effective strategy is to gradually raise awareness through a persistent sharing of newer information and a show- and-tell approach. If you ask the customer to gather all the information and then expect to start configuration, the likelihood of getting started soon automatically goes down. Alternately, minimize requests sent to the customer, go with what you have, make assumptions, note them, enable configurations to change them later, demonstrate a prototype or proof of concept, and then validate assumptions with the customer. As the customer contacts see and interact with the emerging solution, you will trigger their imagination, excitement, and passionate collaboration with the solution.

Your customer points of contact need to continuously make a business case internally to collect critical information from their colleagues. They will likely struggle to get that information, since the talk tracks you provided may not be as clear to them as to you. Follow up your verbal tracks in writing, so that they can refer to it and forward as appropriate. Try to anticipate and reduce resistance they might face internally.

Large customer organizations have a command structure with multiple layers of communication. Manager reports to director, who reports to vice president and so on. Every decision may require multiple approvals and could take longer. Customer service managers need to accordingly tailor their talk tracks, plan to work with, explain, and get buy in from multiple customer executive levels.

Be patient with newer customer recruits and if applicable consulting partner resources. If it takes extra effort to train them, make that extra effort. While you live and breathe your software solution every day, they do not. Don't get frustrated and worse, show that frustration in front of the customer resource. If the skill set required of the customer or partner resource is not adequate, mention that privately to the project sponsor.

Lastly, while vendor is motivated in anticipation of the financial windfall, the customer is looking for value from the implementation and resulting recognition from driving that value within their organization. Make the customer contacts heroes in the eyes of their peers within their organization. Strive to get them awards and recognition for their work on the project.

All these methods will help you get the required attention from the customer and help tide through project management challenges within the customer organization. You will end up making friends who will remain your strong supporters, not only while they are with the customer but also at their future employers.

Superior customer success skills become super important in such situations. Your sales and project management skills outlined earlier in this chapter will enable you to get the required resources from both the vendor and customer end and be successful in your projects.

KEY TAKEAWAYS

The vendor is expected to do more always

Minimize asks of the customer—they are always stretched thin

Handling Customer Objections

Customers raise objections when they interact with vendors throughout all customer touchpoint phases outlined in this book. I cover the key objections relevant to customer success in this phase. As a reminder, only after a contractual agreement is signed with the customer to implement a solution, the customer vendor relationship is formally defined.

Starting with the first interaction with the customer contacts, it is important for the vendor to get their ducks in the row prior to the first call with the vendor. First impressions are important, and your responses will determine your involvement in the project or even the continued health of the project. Always be alert in front of customers. Savvy customer contacts may start with a few curveballs to test the vendor resources assigned to their project, via essentially interview style questioning. Customer questions could be very subtle, and vendor resources may not realize that they are being interviewed.

Vendors should inventory potential objections and document management approved responses. For instance, regarding a question, "how long will it take to deploy the solution?", most vendors should and typically respond with "we are staffed to complete the project in as less as XX weeks if the customer is ready with all of the information required to complete the project."

Experienced customers already understand that most projects take much longer than this baseline, since the time lapse to collect the information and iterate through the system setup is naturally a time-consuming activity.

There should be a central voice that coordinates all responses from the vendor side. Implementation talk tracks should be discussed and agreed by vendor side executives prior to the customer calls.

If there are gaps between the expectations set during sales process and vendor's true capabilities, this information should be relayed by vendor management to the customer success and implementation managers ahead of time. I don't recommend vendors pursue aggressive business practices, by promoting features that don't exist (also called "vapor ware") since they invariably lead to customer heartburn, vendor resource attritions and project delays. In such events, customers force their vendors to eat up significant implementation costs or build the features at vendor's cost or compensate the customer through other means.

It is likely that expectations can be reset with alternate and acceptable solutions. I cover selling and influencing capabilities in the next "Selling Never Stops" section. These capabilities will enable you to get the appropriate buy in, attention and resources for alternate solutions, helping you address these potential objections.

Following are just a few of the numerous objections, questions, and concerns that could come your way during your meetings with the customer.

- "How long will it take to rollout the solution to my end users?"
- "We were led to believe that our involvement on the project will be very less, but here we are asked to assign many full time equivalent (FTE) resources on the project!"
- "Asks from you (the vendor) are unreasonable!"
- "Per sales discussions, the requested information, designs, prep work should have been handled by the vendor."

- "The software interface and capabilities shared today are markedly different from the ones shown during the sales process!"
- "The end user training involvement is very high whereas we were told that the user-friendly nature of the system will not need user training!"
- "Quality of vendor resources is questionable." "They don't seem to be prepared for meetings and struggle through their talk tracks!"
- "There are multiple requests coming in from varied vendor resources with no streamlined central point!"
- Lastly, "our priorities have changed, or the project is delayed."

KEY TAKEAWAYS

Prepare potential objection lists with documented management approved responses

Be alert and prepared to convey a strong positive first impression during implementation kickoff meetings

Selling Never Stops

Contract ratification doesn't automatically smooth the ride for the vendor. Numerous hurdles still need to be addressed before the next contract renewal. Customers intentionally reduce the renewal time to test the vendor and its software solution.

It is incumbent on the vendor resources involved, under the leadership of the CSM to pave the way from this point on and in the next two phases. Sales account representative who got the deal to this stage will look for upsell and cross-sell opportunities and are dependent on these vendor resources to turn the account into a successful reference and continued buyer of the vendor's solutions. The CSMs are and should be part sales professionals to continue the selling process. They need to be polite, patient, persistent, diplomatic, and 100% wedded to the success of the project.

On the customer's end, contacts involved in the sales process may not be the same as earmarked for implementation and deployment. Due to attrition and reorganizations, customer personnel could be reassigned, bringing in new faces and voices that may not have the full perspective, incentives, or the motivation of the original group. Further, customer contacts typically have top competing ten to fifty tasks at a given time and their priorities may change constantly for your project.

It is easy to get frustrated with the slow pace. Against these odds, CSMs need to stay on top, work with the client's pace, and balance their time with other customer projects. If the project makes sense and is compelling, it will bubble up in priority sooner than later. Most vendors assign several customers per CSM based on this expected pace of response and execution speed. In this setup, keep yourself motivated with projects that excite you and have customers' commitment and time. There is usually an interesting customer project in your assigned customer list that will keep you, as CSM or implementation manager, excited and engaged in your roles.

Your influencing capabilities become critical to moving your tasks to the top of the queue. By default, a show-and-tell approach works the best. The sooner you can help realize proof of concepts, show progress, implement faster with minimal help from the customer the better. Just talk will not help and will likely push your tasks and projects to the bottom of the customer contacts' to-do list.

KEY TAKEAWAYS

Don't assume the project will continue after contract ratification

Customer success and implementation manager need to be part sales professionals to drive the project forward

Appreciation of Sales Process

Young customer success and implementation managers may not appreciate the effort and opportunity provided by the salesperson to lead the implementation process. It is important for vendor implementation resources to understand that a lot of stakeholders' time, numerous touchpoints, and investments were required to provide them this opportunity. I recommend exposing customer success and implementation managers to at least one complete sales cycle and the related progress from one stage to another: from sales lead, to opportunity, to demonstration, to RFP response, to contract negotiation, and to closure. This will help them appreciate their role more, and their employer's business better. With a strong understanding of the proposed value presented during the sales process, they will be much more able to realize that value for their customers.

KEY TAKEAWAY

With a strong understanding of the proposed value presented during the sales process, customer success and implementation managers will be much more able to realize that value for their customers

Customer Guide

As a buyer and potential adopter of technology, the customer contacts look for guidance from vendors during implementation conversations. During the sales phase, they have sat through a few product demonstrations and would have formulated opinions about your product, but don't have clear visibility of the implementation roadmap. Vendor resources taking the lead during implementation conversations should be prepared adequately to take the customer guide role. Vendor resources need to be trained, both in theory and practice, and completely conversant with the implemented solution's quirks, nuts and bolts, before they take on the guide role during an implementation.

Before you teach others, make sure you understand exactly what you are teaching. I have seen numerous failed implementations when insufficiently trained vendor resources are given customer-facing roles. Before taking on customer-facing roles, such individuals should implement the solution themselves, either in a sandbox with as realistic real-life data as possible, or better still, have implemented, deployed, and realized success at another customer. The more individual success stories you can experience yourself, the better. It will help you establish and leverage credibility in all your future implementations.

KEY TAKEAWAY

Before you teach others, make sure you understand exactly what you are teaching

Customer Engagement Protocols and Learnings

Vendors may need to spend significant time at customer sites or telecommuting. It is therefore prudent to touch on a few important considerations in this bonding phase. While a certain interaction approach may be acceptable at one customer, that same approach may not be appreciated at others. The size of the customer organization typically influences accepted practice.

At the onset of the engagement, convey to your customer that you are conscious of customer end protocols and would like to be advised of them as and when relevant. Protocols are tied to an organization's culture. Employees observe, ask, learn, and follow protocols customarily at their respective organizations, after being with the same organization for many months, years, or decades. Vendor personnel's interaction time with customer organizations is much limited in comparison and they may need to be apprised of relevant protocols explicitly. These protocols could be seemingly insignificant such as requiring page numbers, font size and type in every customer-facing documentation or presentation. Others could be chain of communication and meeting set up-related protocols. For example, the decision to cancel a meeting involving multiple customer resources may require explicit and strict approval from customer contact, even if another key customer stakeholder has agreed to cancel the meeting.

For customer meetings, be aware and follow the elements outlined in the namesake Chapter 12. Likewise, the elements outlined in Chapter 14 titled "Professional Growth Suggestions" will also help you put your best foot forward.

In addition, always focus on executing your work successfully with minimal distractions. Participate in as few meetings as possible but do stay informed about other areas of the project and company operations.

Always be in continuous learning mode. Observe new technologies, processes, policies, and procedures, and share them with your colleagues in your own organization. This will increase visibility for you and help your vendor organization serve your customers better.

KEY TAKEAWAYS

Take your customer contact's guidance to understand and follow customer end interaction protocols

Always be in continuous learning mode

Avoid distractions and stay focused on your assigned tasks

Stay informed about other areas of the project and operations

Customer Touchpoint Frequency

Right after a software solution is sold, there is natural eagerness and pressure from all stakeholders to implement and deploy the solution. Most contracts are written to realize implementations faster. The vendor is naturally engaged actively and incented to realize this end goal sooner than later.

For project coordinators, I suggest putting an indefinitely reoccurring weekly status meeting on the calendar to review project progress on a weekly basis. The presence of this meeting on the calendar will keep all stakeholders on point till the implementation is complete. It is okay to repurpose the meeting for execution-related conversations. Of course, after the project success is realized, the reoccurring meeting can be deleted.

Billing

Nobody likes surprises. Billing procedures should be clearly defined such that all bills are tied to approved statements of work. CSMs should bill for approved and incurred professional hours only with adequate documentation. They need to set and meet expectations on billable hours. If CSMs expect to go over a certain budget, they need to make sure the customer is aware ahead of time. Results count, not level of effort. CSMs should measure and present bottom-line impact when sending billing statements. Help the customer make a business case not only during project approval but also at time of billing. The customer contact's manager will always ask at time of approving invoice "did we get what we expected." Keep them prepared with appropriate talk tracks to make their job easier and to help represent you well with internal stakeholders.

PLANNING AND DESIGN

The "measure twice, cut once" expression cannot be more appropriate for this section. Best executed projects have a vivid understanding of the desired result, are well thought through and account for all potential loose ends before they are undertaken. In this section I cover technical, usability, product, and functional design considerations in addition to on-ground project management activities.

Project Management

Borrowing from Wikipedia's definition, "Project management is the practice of initiating, planning, executing, controlling, and closing the work of a team to achieve specific goals and meet specific success criteria at the specified time." This book emphasizes the importance of this activity but doesn't attempt to cover this topic holistically. Readers are encouraged to look up other resources to educate themselves fully about this topic. I call out the salient points that have stood out for me during my implementations over a two decade plus career. While technical details of project management can be procured from other sources, this "white hair" wisdom outlined here may not be as clearly and succinctly stated in other sources. Refer to the "People" section in Chapter 2 for a listing of all vendor personae involved in customer success activities in context of this section.

The key responsibility of any customer-facing individual or a resource providing a service is to set and to meet expectations. These are typically the time duration, effort, and resources in terms of hours and cost. Vendor project managers collect this information from each resource tied to the project, aggregate all tasks and streamline them into a project plan. A project plan along with supporting collateral is a means to document the project goals, milestones, activities leading to these milestones, and ownership with buffers for potential slippage. It is a means to outline best-, worst-case scenarios, and mitigation measures so that everyone is aware of and can plan for their individual next steps down the line.

It is the responsibility of the vendor CSM, or others under the leadership of the CSM, to anticipate all possible issues that could occur on the project, i.e. before they occur, and plan accordingly. This planning step includes procurement of tools—technology, infrastructure, and the set-up of a project governance team with escalation touchpoints both at customer and vendor levels. Risks that cannot be mitigated need to be called out, so that everyone can accept them as they are or not take on the project. In a nutshell, the customer success lead, collectively with the implementation manager, is expected to have a vision far out in the future and help the customer contact visualize that vision in the beginning of the project.

After setting these expectations, respectively assigned vendor resources are expected to realize conveyed expectations gradually and surely. A key aspect of delivery management is boosting credibility with small wins. Customer contacts get nervous when milestone dates are not met. This goes back to the setting expectation responsibility. Be less ambitious in the beginning phases. Promise less and do more. Interestingly, this is all in your hands. These small tricks can make or break your projects.

After this initial but key establishing-credibility phase, stay on schedule for all active projects. Projects tend to get off schedule when complacency gets in. Always have indefinite, reoccurring, meetings till the implementation is complete, solution is deployed, and success realized.

KEY TAKEAWAYS

Set and meet expectations

Anticipate, plan and socialize risks with stakeholders

Build credibility with small wins

Stay on schedule with indefinite, reoccurring touchpoint meetings

Simplicity in Implementations

The goal of every implementation should be seamless deployment of the solution across the user community. End users don't have the time to learn new technologies, interfaces, and processes. They have their own job to worry about, and most new optional asks of them typically fall on deaf ears. If something is designed to improve their lives and is simple to adopt, they will be all ears.

The solution should accordingly be usable, maintainable and administrable. Don't over complicate implementations. Personality types that have the intrinsic need to be challenged tend to over analyze requirements and end up complicating the solution. Watch for this behavior in yourself or your customer side counterparts.

It is much easier to scale with these principles. "The Economics of Software as a Solution Software (SaaS) Deployments" section in Chapter 1 covers the financial windfalls of a sound implementation.

KEY TAKEAWAYS

Don't over complicate implementations

Watch for personality types on your team that like to over analyze requirements

Intuitive implementation that make end users' lives easier and fruitful will achieve the most success

Design Review

All requirements and designs should be routed through a committee of experts, product managers or solution architects to make sure that the design is blessed across the organization. Keep your ego aside if you think you are the expert and don't need others buy in. Make project success the full organization's responsibility. Toe the official company line and strive for utmost transparency so that everyone as a group can watch for project risks and plan mitigation measures collectively.

Approach to the contrary will likely be at your own risk. If the project fails, you will be on the hook. As investigation measure, your peers will request copies of all emails, notes, and documentation, putting you in the defensive position. Typically, after two or three failed projects, most CSMs and relevant vendor resources are asked to move on. So, don't push your luck.

Product Limitations—Avoid Saying "No" to Requested Features

No enterprise software product is perfect. They are designed to work with numerous customers, and therefore, are set up with baseline functionalities. Configurations, and in seldom cases, customizations are required to align functionality with customer requirements. Configuring the most appropriate solution is the collective responsibility of customer success and implementation managers.

Sometimes, customer contacts get adventurous and attempt to configure vendor's application on their own, without adequate training, for their requirements. When they encounter difficulties, they inquire about functionality that may or may not be necessary for the implementation. When this requested functionality doesn't exist, customer success and implementation managers may find themselves in a spot. That brings up the question, "when to and when not to say 'no,' when vendors don't have the requested functionality."

The word "no" clearly has a negative connotation and pushes a potential buyer or adopter of your product away from you. Keeping the prospect or recently signed customer engaged during such tricky conversations is an important responsibility of these two roles.

A categorical "No" is better when a "yes" answer will cause the customer to be intentionally misled and will be a blatant lie. But when the question or functionality is irrelevant to the implementation, you can avoid saying "no" while staying honest to your customer.

You can and should avoid saying "No" when a better alternative exists or can be made available at short notice. Remember you are the solution expert. Prepare your word tracks accordingly. For instance, you can start with "we have been implementing this solution for XX years" or "numerous customers have asked for this functionality, however they have soon realized that the alternative approach is much more intuitive in the context of your requirements."

KEY TAKEAWAY

Don't mislead your customers, however, when a better solution exists or can be made available, you can avoid answering a customer's question with a black and white "no" answer

Product Enhancement Ideas

Customer interactions trigger and are a significant source of worthwhile product enhancement ideas. I touch on the product management topic here, since new feature ideas typically originate during implementation planning sessions, and it is valuable for both customer experience and customer success needs.

If you play a product manager role in addition to your customer success responsibilities, don't ask customers how a feature should be designed. Designing is product manager's job, and moreover you don't want the feature to be specific to just one customer. Ask for feedback on alpha or beta version instead, if the customer proactively offers to help with this request. For consulting projects, where the solution is specific to just one customer, this recommendation may not apply.

In a product manager's role, stay creative and always look for newer ideas, efficiencies, and processing techniques. Go beyond theoretical, irrespective of the company or technology you are representing. Constantly experiment, configure, implement, and program in a sandbox or at an actual client implementation. It is much easier to narrate experiences gathered from experimentation, or actual customer implementations and thereby demonstrate credibility in front of your customers.

I cover "Demonstrating Business Value of Implemented Solutions" section in Chapter 9, titled "Adopt." Suffice it to say for now that your products should be deployable and should add business value to your customers.

KEY TAKEAWAYS

Listen to your customers, if they offer feedback and ideas

Product design and user experience is your responsibility if you play a product manager's role. Don't let customers box you into something specific for that customer

Be creative, think out of the box, and build to scale

EXECUTION

With adequate planning, execution becomes much simpler and straightforward. Resources are requested to execute as agreed and report back to the project manager who then communicates status to all relevant stakeholders. As mentioned in Part I introduction, domain-specific knowledge or guidance is out of scope of this book. In the execution subphase, industry, product, and domain knowledge rise in prominence. Training materials cover product or industry-specific information in addition to customer specific configurations in the information technology solution. Keeping the soft skills point of view as focus, I touch on a couple of viewpoints for this phase.

Implementation Training

Enterprise implementations require involvement of a significant user base at customer sites. If the solution is not trivial and requires preparation and delivery of extensive training materials, training all users becomes a significant undertaking. A tree approach where a few champion trainers are trained first, who then train a few more potential trainers each is one option. However, this is subject to the learning and training capabilities of the trained trainers. Alternative solution would be for vendor's trainers to train as many users directly.

Training could be delivered through web meeting sessions, video conferencing, or via in-person classroom-style sessions. For the latter, trainers fly into multiple user locations where users could be grouped into locally accessible training locations. If in-person sessions are preferred, this approach turns out to be cost-effective and efficient for all stakeholders involved.

Continuous Customer Engagement

It is generally a good idea to get every opportunity to speak with the customer contact, especially after a key milestone. Interim updates can be shared by email in respect of everyone's time. Continually make and show incremental progress while managing customer's time and level of interest. Accordingly, schedule meetings that aggregate enough talking points to convey to customers.

Continuous engagement is important across all customer touchpoint phases. As I transition to the next phases, rollout and adoption, note that these time periods especially require regular follow ups. It is important to regularly measure testing and production usage, get continuous feedback and course correct to truly realize the goals of the implementation.

Reach out to your customers informally and occasionally, if you have a good relationship with them. At the very least, schedule periodic touchpoint meetings, formal adoption sessions, in advance for the full year which is the topic of the Adopt phase covered in chapter 9.

KEY TAKEAWAY

Touch base with your customer, often, but not more than what the customer finds valuable in these meetings

8

ROLLOUT

BUILDING AND CONFIGURING A SOLUTION, as executed in the implementation phase and as accepted by customer's management, is only half the battle. Getting it out to the masses, i.e. end users, is the other equally significant undertaking and shouldn't be overlooked or understaffed during the planning phases of the project. Instead of a flow diagram, I will represent the sequential activities in this phase as a list, supported by descriptions, to achieve the same effect.

ACTIVITY:
Training

Description: Vendors leverage standardized training materials to tailor them for the customer specific configurations. This material includes user guides, configuration specific screenshots, quizzes, hands on activities related to the deployed application, check-lists and supporting presentations. Training is typically subdivided into administration and end-user sessions.

End-user training is delivered by vendors to customer champions, influencers and as many end-users that vendors can train on their own. Geographically distributed and language-specific influencers and champions train the rest of the multilingual community if applicable. Administration-specific training is delivered to customer points of contact who will be taking the administration role such as for adding users, updating configurations, and reviewing usage.

ACTIVITY:
User Acceptance Test (UAT)

Description: Customer influencers and champions execute all administrative and end-user activities in the implemented vendor solution. Taking attendance time sheet software as an example, this testing team will test administrative steps such as to add employees and consultants using the system, set up the number of holidays in a year, configure regular and overtime hourly rates by resource type and expense categories. End-user steps will be submitting timecards and expense reimbursement requests.

ACTIVITY:
Pilot Rollout

Description: Before requiring all end users to use the application in practice, a few representative ones are asked to test and apply vendor's software for production scenarios. If, for instance, the software is applicable for submitting attendance time sheets, may be 5% of the users are first asked to use the software for submitting their daily time sheets in addition to their regular approach to submitting the same. The redundancy helps compare existing environment and results with the post-software scenario. Once results are satisfactorily validated, another pilot could be pursued or the full scale rollout depending on management's comfort level with the new solution.

ACTIVITY:
Onboarding

Description: Post training, end users are provided login information, secured access to their areas of responsibility, checklists, and cheat sheets for pinup on end-user desks.

ACTIVITY:
Monitoring

Description: Administrators check system usage, collect feedback from end users, confirm realization of desired value. Senior customer staff escalate issues with the vendor CSM if results and benefits are unsatisfactory.

ACTIVITY:
Vendor Follow-Up

Description: CSM follows up periodically with customer contacts to ensure rollout activities are progressing on customer end. They reinforce deployed vendor products' value proposition through customer specific marketing literature and talk tracks.

As with rest of this book, I will only touch on the high-level activities in this phase to emphasize the importance of each activity but won't attempt to cover each activity holistically. Readers are encouraged to look up other resources to educate themselves fully about each activity. Most vendor's training materials offer details on each of the activities above.

A good rollout is critical to adoption but distinct from it. Only attempt to rollout what is adoptable. Admittedly, the following sections overlap the implementation and adoption phases. I have elaborated these sections here to highlight their importance as you pursue rollout activities. The sections contain the salient points and soft skill considerations that have stood out for me in this phase.

ADOPTABILITY OF SOLUTION

Workplace software or a workplace hardware product is not unlike any end-consumer product in terms of user acceptance. People accept products such as clothing, furniture, electronics, or appliances only if they appreciate the combination of aesthetics, value, utility, and ease of use of the product. We all know that as end consumers we cannot be forced to buy or use the product. The same principles apply in the workplace. Senior management cannot enforce usage, if a software solution, office hardware (such as copiers or laptops), or furniture doesn't offer utility, ease of use, or aesthetics to end users of the product.

When workplace solutions or products are rolled out, vendors tend to collect commitments from management or product champions that the customer will commit to use the product. These commitments are typically of limited value and teeth, if the product is not inherently appealing to end users. While it is important to adequately make end users aware of a product's capabilities and to appropriately train them, the product itself should be designed to be "adoptable" by end users.

PRODUCT STICKINESS AND MARKETING

Vendors are also advised to look for "stickiness" in their product implementations so that the product cannot be uprooted easily in the future. This stickiness can be instituted at customer locations via integrations with customer's other systems, scale of adoption and acceptance by many users. Rollout activity will accordingly involve testing seamless integration, confirming ease of use and scalability of the solution.

Marketing is an important skill when engaging with a large user community. Convincing each user directly to engage with the solution is not realistic. CSMs should leverage recorded verbal and written mass communication pieces to continually emphasize the importance, and benefits of the solution, in collaboration with customer's core team comprised of project managers, influencers and champions. All communications should be vetted thoroughly with relevant stakeholders, tested with a smaller audience before distribution to the larger audience.

Continuous and relevant communications are important in the post-rollout phases as well to maintain awareness of the vendor's products. Out of sight/out of mind is a critical risk, that vendors should always watch for and remediate.

SUCCESS BREEDS SUCCESS

Maintain relationships with product champions who have been engaged throughout the implementation process. Serve their needs and address their feedback promptly. Celebrate their success with the product in all possible forums. Make them the hero in their respective groups and organizations. Work with them to document case studies, record videos, and prepare presentations. Help promote this collateral on customer's knowledge-sharing applications.

Look for winning techniques that help them be more productive, effective, efficient, and successful at their jobs. Ensure they have access to up-to-date training materials to share with their colleagues and peers. Help them spread the word and get you more license revenue.

Success breeds success. Strive for frictionless adoption. Suggest and remove hurdles in People, Process and System areas as highlighted in Chapter 2.

KEY TAKEAWAYS

Strive for frictionless rollout by fine-tuning all three aspects of implementations—people, process, and systems

Celebrate end-user wins

Help the customer spread the word and help you gain traction across their larger user community

CHANGE MANAGEMENT

Changing any aspect of an employee's workplace is a significant undertaking. Making the person change their daily schedule or activity is akin to changing someone's habit. It takes effort to socialize the need, educate, initiate, and monitor usage patterns till a new habit is created in the workplace. Any visualized change needs to be well thought through before it is considered for application in the workplace.

Project coordinators need to watch for both overt and covert pushback. They need to prepare responses ahead of time for all potential objections from end users. Both tangible and intangible benefits should be identified ahead of time, in addition to potential incentives that are meaningful to end users.

A change management plan should be clearly documented and shared with all relevant stakeholders. The people, process and systems framework could be used to identify dependencies across these three interconnected elements. Each potential issue or risk should be explored, discussed, and documented. Mitigating solutions should accordingly be identified in addition to executing scenario analysis to identify all possible outcomes. Senior management should be presented with a holistic risk framework so that they take on the overall change management risk with eyes wide open. Typically, management at this stage, either accepts the risk as is, accepts reduced risk after investing in mitigating solutions, transfers the risk to a third-party, or avoids the risk by not taking on change management at this stage. In simple terms, using the timesheet application example at an industrial organization, management could decide to move forward with the software's deployment across all of its employees, could deploy to only a subset employee base, could transfer software based timesheet responsibility to another third-party or could decide to stay with the current procedures.

If the stakeholders decide to move forward with the change management initiative, periodic progress is monitored, shared with affected stakeholders and reported to senior management. At appropriate project milestones, management continuously tracks risk landscape, and makes a call to proceed, risk adjust, or abort based on the information received on project coordinators.

KEY TAKEAWAYS

Any visualized change needs to be well thought through before it is considered for application in the workplace

Project coordinators need to prepare responses ahead of time for all potential objections from end users and watch for both overt and covert pushback

9

ADOPT

ONLY WHEN A PRODUCT IS woven into the fabric of an organization and translated into a naturally understood value, will it find adoption. The activities covered in the previous phases lay a solid foundation for the users to start using the system. In the adopt phase, ongoing onboarding, training, and usage is happening on the customer end. End users use relevant aids to train, use, and get familiar with the system. From a vendor standpoint, CSMs have and should have done everything to set the right expectations and execute accordingly. In this phase, they need to be around to provide support, clarifications, make minor adjustments to the configuration, and actively monitor usage. There is a possibility that the setup is not optimal, in which case, customer interaction may revert to implementation phase to get everything right.

My coverage of this phase is focused on vendor's continuous monitoring, periodic encouragement, value emphasis, course correction and business development, so that CSMs can solidify and grow their business with the customer.

Key Stakeholders and Activities

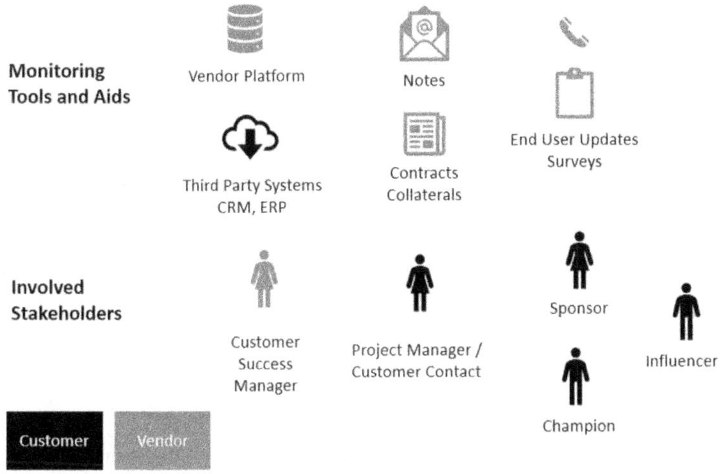

Figure 9.1: Adopt Phase: Involved Resources and Stakeholders

After rolling out a solution to the end users, both vendor and customer stakeholders need to proactively monitor progress. Once users adopt the product and integrate with daily activities, customer retention becomes a straightforward exercise.

For this phase, I will use a combination of visual and supporting sequential (and iterative) activity list to describe the elements here. Relevant parties are advised to keep iterating over these activities to achieve desired success. After the activity and relevant personae responsibility outline, I will focus on the key behavioral considerations to make CSM and the vendor successful. The Appendices contain several checklists, formats, meeting agenda suggestions that can be leveraged for executing the activities in this phase.

Elements outlined in Part I of this book, will help the readers acquaint with the monitoring tools and aids required to measure success. A vendor's own cloud or on-premise platform, along with third-party systems integrated with the vendor's platform, will provide information on usage and realized metrics. Deployed survey responses will collect qualitative feedback from end users using or trying to use the system. Contract collaterals, user notes will provide desired goals of the project. Given the magnitude of this information a customer success software solution will help streamline this data set.

Vendor resources led by a CSM will work with customer end personnel such as project coordinators, administrators, sponsors, influencers, and champions as outlined in following table.

ACTIVITY:
Periodic Informal Touchbase

Description: Success manager schedules periodic informal touchpoint meetings with customer contact.

ACTIVITY:
Informal feedback

Description: CSM requests inputs from champions, and customer contact.

ACTIVITY:
Feedback Survey Deployment

Description: CSM deploys feedback surveys to friendly end users, champions in collaboration with customer contact.

ACTIVITY:
Outcome (Goal) Management

Description: CSM reviews contracts, objectives, implementation meeting notes, objectives, last meeting recordings and notes.

ACTIVITY:
Formal Quarterly (Periodic) Business Reviews

Description: CSM schedules formal business review meetings between vendor senior management and key customer personae such as sponsor, influencer and project coordinator to review progress and alignment with desired goals. For this meeting, there is attention to gathering all relevant success metrics derived from systems in Figure 9.1 and as described in Chapter 4 titled "Success Measurement Tools." Senior executives expect thorough preparation before this meeting.

ACTIVITY:
Reference / Recommendation Requests

Description: Once customer satisfaction is established CSM reaches out to customer contacts and friendly champions for both formal and informal recommendations such as through testimonials, joint case studies, and reference calls / meetings with prospects.

ACTIVITY:
Upsell, Cross-Sell, and New License Business Development

Description: Exploring opportunistic times, CSM suggests, tests waters, and proposes additional business development ideas to customer contacts. To reiterate a point made earlier in the book, smart customers don't mind investing more if there is continuous and incremental value in vendors' solutions.

High-Level Adoption Challenges

Like the implementation phase flow diagram above, I touch on a few challenges below to lay the groundwork for the rest of the chapter. Activities described above are aspirational and don't always receive favorable response from customer contacts. Convincing ability of the CSM is key to handling these activities. Guidance provided in the rest of this phase chapter will help you think through and prepare situation specific remedies for these and other challenges outlined herewith. Technical and efficiency challenges in collecting and managing data are best handled with automated customer success solutions.

1. Lack of customer contact's interest in sharing data from third-party systems, or in calling end users
2. Lack of continuity in conversation due to missed meetings, missing notes and incomplete action items
3. Broken relationships due to turn over on either end
4. Time-consuming effort to collect data, streamline, and to prepare consistent presentation materials
5. Difficulty in tracking relevant sources of information
6. Non standardized and ad hoc processes for collecting data

PRODUCT USE

When end users using the system cannot operate without vendors' solutions, and when they see productivity gains, time savings, revenue boosts, mitigated risks and cost savings, adoption becomes automatic. New users become interested in the solution, after seeing their peers using the solution. New implementation ideas are generated resulting in asks for additional licenses. Smart vendors cost effectively scale their platforms and implementations, for these additional licenses that don't require much additional effort from their end, further boosting returns.

The above scenario is more aspirational and may not always turn out dead right. In every project there are numerous moving parts, and dependencies on multiple third-party providers, such as Internet browsers, operating systems and databases, on which a vendor solution is built. Software version issues with any of these inter-related systems could result in usability, performance and scalability concerns affecting adoption success. If the vendor's solution is essential for customer's operations, end users will maintain patience. Vendor and customer resources should pursue appropriate communication strategies and work toward collaboratively addressing these technical difficulties.

On the flip side, nice to have projects, that don't capture the imagination of the end users, struggle to succeed. Vendors may influence end users' managers to encourage usage, but that may become a losing battle. Such vendors keep trying to iterate the configuration setup on their own dime every few months and quarters, negatively affecting returns. Vendor's resources, typically CSMs and sales personnel, spend disproportionate time on continued customer contact outreach—such as via in person visits, phone calls and or emails, not to mention the time investment in generating supporting marketing and sales materials. License renewals at this point may not be worth the effort on both sides and may result in eventual terminations.

Level of effort to put in during these situations is largely tied to the vendor's conviction in their products. Additionally, decision to abort or stay engaged requires business judgment by vendor's leadership team. The results could be positive too. Practical vendors have a vision for the future that may not be ready for the current times. Number of successful vendors today, struggled to get their products out in the market during the first round. Building on the motivational theory, one can make a business case for try and try till you succeed. In such a visionary scenario, customer success managers are advised to continually engage end users, measure deployment, gather feedback, course correct, fine-tune and repeat iteratively. This also ties back to the section titled "Selling Never Stops" covered in Chapter 7 "Implementation Phase." CSMs are part sales professionals and need to carry on the responsibility of the sales professional, after the first contract with the customer is signed. In the best-case circumstances, when the timing is right, vendor makes technological advances, industry generally accepts the solution encouraging the customer, and there is availability of complementary solutions, vendor will taste success. CSM's contributions and successes in such adversities will be widely appreciated across the vendor and customer organizations.

KEY TAKEAWAYS

Meaningful undertakings generate profitable returns through year over year renewals

Technical challenges and other hiccups associated with essential solutions should be handled with appropriate communication and collaboration with relevant parties

Nice to have projects struggle to gain traction and eventually fade away

Persistent efforts should be supported by sound business judgment. If something is not meant to be, it is not meant to be, at the same time visionary endeavors do succeed

REALIZE VALUE AND BROADCAST VALUE

Overall goal behind every adoption is ensuring desired outcomes are met. Once creditworthy evidence is collected to validate realized value by and for customer, companies should invest in marketing collateral to broadcast generated value across all customer stakeholders and end users. The same or variations of this collateral can also augment company's sales and marketing collateral for augmenting ongoing business development initiatives.

Clear articulation of realized value, will open the possibility of additional revenue from the customer, via upsell and cross-sell opportunities. Former encourages the customer to upgrade to higher value product or larger number of licenses. Latter encourages the customer to purchase complementary products from the vendor. If not additional value, customer will at least commit to renew licenses. Customer success professionals are advised to always explore multiyear licenses after demonstration of realized value. Multiyear licenses will boost the value of the company in the eyes of company investors while reducing the risk of premature customer loss.

Multiyear license arrangements however shouldn't result in complacency. Customer success professionals should always put their best foot forward in continuously engaging multiyear contract customers. There are always additional benefits that can be obtained from delighted customers such as reference calls, joint case studies in addition to ongoing upsell and cross-sell opportunities. The caveat "out of sight/out of mind" should be an important reminder for all CSMs.

DEMONSTRATING BUSINESS VALUE OF IMPLEMENTED SOLUTIONS

Software as a service (SAAS) deployments have made it easier for customers to switch. Vendors' failure to demonstrate value can result in premature terminations or affect incremental license revenue.

Project sponsors need talk tracks to justify continued investments in vendor solutions. The chief financial officer's (CFO) office or sponsors' bosses will invariably ask for this justification at same point or the other, most likely during renewals. For every significant and incremental cost, CFOs need justifiable and meaningful business case presentations. Sponsors don't have the time or resources internally for this effort, feel that it is the responsibility of the vendor to compute and provide this value. Vendor should collaboratively determine this value for the sponsor's organization, document and streamline into appealing presentations, for the CFO team and others in the customer organization.

Identifying quantifiable hard cost savings, productivity gains, revenue gains or risk mitigation is hard. Customer success leads should start with data resident in their own systems to extrapolate realized business value. Additionally, request customers to provide information retained in customer relationship management (CRM), enterprise risk management (ERP), human resources (HR), or risk management solutions to further support your generated value narrative.

KEY TAKEAWAYS

Proactively provide your solution's business case talk tracks to your project sponsor

This will help them justify the solution internally and facilitate renewals

TRACKING ADOPTION THROUGH QUARTERLY BUSINESS REVIEWS (QBR)

Choose the frequency of quarterly business reviews (QBR) meetings based on the nature of the business, customer specific situation and your availability. Assess your customer lists and group them by in-implementation and post deployment lists. Give time for adoption after implementations before you schedule adoption meetings for in-implementation accounts. For latter, plan to touch base every quarter, although the frequency could be higher or lower depending on the situation. Too frequent calls with just deployed customers may make these calls ineffective. Availability of resources in the customer success group, full- vs.

part-time resource status in the customer success function and customer availability will also play a role in allotting time for these meetings.

Request clients to collect adoption metrics, captured in other third-party systems (as suggested in previous section) such as customer relationship management, enterprise risk management, HR or risk management solutions, ahead of these meetings. This data is a goldmine for your sales and marketing teams who are always eager to get their hands on it. Play your cards well. Don't persist annoyingly if there is no response. Be polite. If you push too much, you may not get much. Typically, the customers that are most successful in deploying this solution, are more forthcoming in giving you this information. Send out adoption assessment questionnaires and usage metric templates. When you incur time in collecting data when none exists, you may get "nothing to say" from customer contacts. On receiving such push backs, don't press further or they will stop taking your calls, damaging the relationships.

Then use this combination of real or extrapolated quantitative and qualitative data to create a perspective, a hypothesized value talk track, on the adoption prior to the quarterly business review meeting. Go with what you have and then validate with the customer. The key is to make the customer's time worthwhile. Add insights, industry perspectives, data, and analysis from other customers' usage. Share product roadmap, which is often of interest to customers to see the type of investments the vendor is making in research, development, and resource augmentation.

Make them feel that they learned something from the interaction. Keep augmenting your bag of information with new industry perspectives, new tools and product extensions. Ask your fellow customer success, sales, implementation, and support teams to do the same.

After the meeting, follow through on action items. Failure to show progress from previous calls will render upcoming ones ineffective and worst case loathed.

KEY TAKEAWAYS

Show generated value from your solutions

Gather data from your system and ask for data from customers' third-party solutions

You may get "nothing to say or share" from customer contacts. On receiving such push backs, don't press further or they will stop taking your calls, damaging the relationships

Make do with you have, and or add other perspectives from comparable implementations

A+ CUSTOMER REFERENCES

Make your customers references. They will not only help you win other accounts but also buy more from you. They are invested in you, so they want to make sure you remain a viable business.

If incremental sales at every customer is organizationally vendor sales executives' responsibility, collaborate with your sales representatives for upsell, cross-sell, and incremental license revenue. Bring them into client locations and expose them to potential sales opportunities. The more people from your organization engage with the customer, the better.

Gifts

Most companies have policies stating that employees cannot receive gifts worth more than $25 from vendors. CSMs will encounter situations where a monetarily insignificant gift may help you convey thanks to your customer contacts. In such situations, even if a gift policy doesn't exist at a customer, stay under the $25 to $40 range when sending gifts to customers.

For genuine thank-you gestures to customers—say for speaking publicly at vendor sponsored events, desserts, such as cupcakes or doughnuts, may be a good idea. It shows appreciation, while allowing the contact to share the dessert, and your company name, with a larger group of customer resources.

Dinners are another option if meeting directly with the customer, or if you are already working with them in person on a periodic basis.

While appreciation gestures such as above are acceptable, enticing users to use vendor's products in return for some monetary value is not a good idea. The product should be worthwhile and adoptable. Some startups encourage adoption by sending say gift cards for ten to twenty-five dollars. I don't recommend this. Your product shouldn't be in a state where usage is actively pushed by customer success managers. Remember, if it is not usable, no matter how many calls or bribes, in form of gift cards, you make or send, end users will not use. You will only manage to get a reluctant acceptance for the time being.

IMPLEMENTATION LEARNINGS

CSM and implementation manager roles should share with customers, learnings from other customers. This include interesting management styles, team setup, reporting structures and meeting cadence that has helped other customers stay on top of their implementations and deployments. CSMs should share this information generously with each other from their own experiences and should be on the continuous look out for this information to have meaningful conversations with customers in upcoming meetings. Are there interesting data crunching, analytical ideas, algorithms, operational, manufacturing processes that could benefit my or other customers? Any new tools, systems, technical innovation of any kind worthy of sharing?

I covered knowledge systems in Chapter 5. Large consulting companies maintain significant document management solutions on the cloud for easy sharing of this collective knowledgebase across the enterprise. Get into the habit of publishing on such platforms regularly. You will automatically increase your profile within your organization and be on track to be an influential leader.

KEY TAKEAWAY

Learn from other engagements and share generously

10

REVIEW AND AUDIT BY CUSTOMER

IN ADDITION TO COLLABORATING WITH each other during adoption phase, vendor and customer stakeholder teams will likely evaluate the project success separately. The same metrics, content, meeting notes, project documentation are used to look back on the project activities to learn for future endeavors. Since this chapter is under Part II, Circular Customer Touchpoint Phases, I have listed here the activities and their descriptions as executed by customers, for review and audit purposes.

Vendor related review and guidance is covered separately and in more detail as part of Part III, Customer Success Team and Operational Considerations.

IMPLEMENTATION REVIEW

Vendor's product is likely a part of a bigger program. Customers will look to see if the broader program objectives are met and accordingly execute these activities in that broader context.

Customer Team Review Activities

ACTIVITY:
End User Feedback

Description: Customer project manager (CPM) may not depend on the feedback collected by vendor and may independently request input from end users via phone, email or formal survey utilities.

ACTIVITY:
Collect Success Metrics

Description: Likewise, CPM may independently collect data from third-party systems and vendor database if needed to verify usage.

ACTIVITY:
Contract Review

Description: CPM reviews contracts, project objectives, and broader program goals to see if they are collectively realized.

ACTIVITY:
Identify and Share Findings (Issues)

Description: CPM identifies and shares findings with stakeholder team.

ACTIVITY:
Audit

Description: For large projects, internal audit teams may execute detailed audits to root cause failures: lack of adoption, budget overruns, skill mismatches and missed expectations to name a few.

ACTIVITY:
Vendor Specific Investment

Description: CPM prepares and presents point of view for contract renewals—increase / decrease licenses or not renew contracts.

ACTIVITY:
Program Investment

Description: CPM makes business case for following-year budget updates.

Review (by Customer) Challenges

Visibility of challenges faced by customers during their own independent review will help CSMs collaborating with them.

1. Lack of adequate tools to collect feedback from end users, especially when user count is high
2. Low value contracts may not get attention and could be consistently over paid and under utilized
3. Availability of staff to process this information
4. Scheduling conflicts with internal stakeholders to drive timely consensus
5. Elapsed auto-renew checkpoint dates resulting in forced payment for unusable questionable value solutions

These challenges may affect a customer's ability to respond to CSM requests. Based on the importance scale of the project, in context of the larger scheme of things, CSMs should align their expectations of customer's time and availability.

IMPLEMENTATION AUDITS

Large implementations are and should be subject to audits by either internal or third-party auditors. This section is not meant to be a detailed study of auditing procedures, and simply highlights the broad areas covered by auditors during such audits.

For readers unfamiliar with auditing procedures, an audit is a collection of questionnaires and testing procedures. Auditors either ask questions, observe, inspect, or analyze data. The series of steps that they follow need to be reviewed by senior auditors. These steps are subdivided into one large Audit test case or broken out into multiple audits. Each audit has a final deliverable report, containing executed procedures, their results, observations and remediation suggestions. Procedures are supported by checklists. Based on the checklist response further testing or data collection may be required.

The role of auditors has changed over the years and are now required to play the role of an independent consultant as well. They no longer just prepare a list of findings, but also outline remediation measures to address implementation gaps. In many cases, they stay on to correct the gaps collaboratively with other consultants. Following the practice followed by large auditing companies, I recommend the People, Process and Systems framework outlined in Chapter 2 for implementation audits.

I recommend that CSM and implementation managers be aware of these audit procedures. Awareness of not only the procedures but also findings, best practices, and remediation measures, will make them savvier during their interactions with their customers.

Audit Using Customer Success Framework

Implementation auditors break down and segment their implementation audit procedures by *people, process, and systems elements.* I share below a few representative audit checklists for each element type. Each auditor prefers to go with their own preferences, internal requirements and historical context, and may follow a slightly different audit methodology.

People

The audit checklist in this section covers team setup, stakeholder, human resources, and political considerations potentially affecting the health of the project:

- Are end users using the solution?
- Were resources qualified to manage the project?
- Were project plans, documentation and issue tracking kept up-to-date adequately?
- For large projects, was a consulting partner knowledgeable about the domain involved?
- Were resources motivated?
- Were resources adequately allotted hours to complete the project?
- Were there conflicts of interest?
- Is the reporting structure adequate?

Process

This checklist covers company operations, policies and procedures, and technical processes:

- Were approval processes followed?
- Were there checks and balances in sharing and processing of data?
- Were privacy concerns addressed?
- (Technical example) Did team use the most optimal algorithm to process data?

System

This checklist covers system features, training, requirements, and infrastructure:

- Were adequate training materials and opportunities provided to end users?
- Were requirements documented and conveyed clearly?
- Is the system right for the perceived solution?

PART III

CUSTOMER SUCCESS TEAM AND OPERATIONAL CONSIDERATIONS

Positive attitude and customer service personality form the bedrock foundation of all successful customer-facing personnel. This part builds on this foundation and covers CSM team mindset, soft skills, vendor side project reviews, supervision, and guidance aspects, required to be successful in CSM initiatives. I outline common sense approaches to performing this role in this book part.

I also provide guidance for CSM senior leadership. It is their responsibility to guide on-ground resources handling day to day customer conversations during tricky situations. These resources will see value in supervisor's feedback, only when latter's ideas and suggestions translate into productive wins and issue resolutions. Supervisor's critical feedback alone for staff may result in a caustic environment and should be avoided.

11

CUSTOMER SUCCESS PERSONA

STRONG RELATIONSHIPS WITH CUSTOMER CONTACTS are central to driving ongoing revenue from customers. This chapter explores customer expectations, CSM skills, approaches and mindset required to be successful in CSM role and to bond with your customer contacts. The person who fills these shoes must keep the customers' needs and expectations in mind, all while applying the outlined skills and approaches and keeping a positive mindset.

CUSTOMER SERVICE MINDSET

The customer success role exists to make the customer successful. Successful leaders understand that they exist because of their customers and will do everything to serve their customers' professional needs. In corporate relationships, one person's success is tied to the other party's success. Customer personae assigned to the project represent the customer, but their individual professional objectives become as important if not more as that of the body represented by them. CSMs should first and foremost watch for their customer contacts' professional needs. When everyone's interests are aligned, projects run smoothly. In the "Process" section of Chapter 2, I highlight six high-level activities that should underpin all interactions with your customers. These activities will ensure achievement of both customer and customer contacts' interests.

Every individual seeks attention. In the CSM role, your job is to provide attention, keeping the focus on the customer. I have seen occasions where vendor resources boast about their own titles, awards, and other achievements. Such actions become unproductive and run counter to the desired effect. Highlight achievements and roles, that are in the interest of the customer and related projects.

When you always remember that your role exists to make the customer successful, you will automatically incorporate the right customer service mindset to incorporate the guidance outlined here.

KEY TAKEAWAYS

The customer success role exists to make the customer successful

You are working with the customer to serve their organization and are paid for that effort; everything else is extraneous

EXPECTATIONS OF A CUSTOMER SUCCESS LEAD

Customers expect their vendor points of contact, especially the ones holding the title of customer success manager or an equivalent position, to be their trusted advisor. A few of the many hats expected to be worn by this person include:

Advocate:

Customers want this person to represent their interests within the vendor's organization, especially when product enhancement requests are submitted by the customer. CSMs should follow through on the enhancement requests, check the feasibility of undertaking these enhancements, and update their customers on the likelihood of addressing these requests. If involved customers are invested in your solution and are trying to suggest enhancements, you owe it to them to provide a fair response to their suggestions and potentially take them on as a research and development effort.

Technical Advisor:

The customer success individual on his or her own, or in consultation with product experts is expected to provide the most optimal solution for customer's needs.

Project Manager:

The customer success contact should be a strong project manager with a go-getter mindset. The person should have executive leverage to push through both vendor and customer end action items. Collaboration, task sequencing, time management, and follow through are important skills to drive project success.

Confidence Booster:

The person should infuse confidence that customer specific requirements have been successfully addressed with other customers by vendor.

Facilitator:

CSM should be socially intelligent, able to lead conversations effectively, bring people together, have good de-escalation skills and defuse heated exchanges or tense situations. The person should respect everyone else's inputs and have a calm demeanor to handle any heated exchange.

Visionary:

CSM should provide a clear vision for execution and progressively lead customers successfully to that projected end state.

Troubleshooter:

It is the job of the customer success manager to anticipate issues before they realize and proactively stop or mitigate them depending on the situation.

Strong Communicator:

Verbal eloquence, coherent thinking, and influential writing skills differentiate an impressive customer success personality from a mediocre one. CSM is a strong listener and observer keeping themselves informed about everything related to the project. They look for visual cues and body language of all project stakeholders when interacting with them.

Trainer:

The CSM loves to learn and then share the knowledge that is acquired with others. This person doesn't shy away from reading and learning about all aspects and perspectives of an industry domain. An educated and informed person comes across as a well-rounded personality and commands respect. They manage the collective representation of vendor's knowledge and expertise by bringing in appropriate resources at relevant times during customer conversations. For instance, during the Rollout phase covered in Chapter 8, CSMs lead the overall training program and bring in technical resources to cover respective technical details.

When customers feel confident that their customer success manager is on top of all things relevant, they automatically become passionate and bind themselves to the successful execution of the project.

KEY TAKEAWAYS

Customers look for a well-rounded personality to manage their relationship with the vendor

The customer needs to know that their concerns have been heard and are being addressed

COMMUNICATION

In every job or career, communication skills are paramount to success. This includes proficiency in the spoken language, in the written word, and in settings that call for public speaking. Command over spoken and written language builds confidence and helps control the outcome of customer interactions. Person who has made the investment in these skill sets, is looked up favorably and offered increasing responsibilities.

Let's dive into the elements that underpin communication skills. I leave out listening skills for now since it is covered throughout this book and focus on message composition, and message delivery. What to convey, when to convey, and how to convey messages are covered in this chapter.

Quality of Thinking and Action

As consumers, when we buy products, we want to buy the ones with quality. Likewise, for services work, if you employ a contractor to work in your house, you want the one that is the most skilled and smartest to guide you through the house project. Similarly, businesses want to employ the smartest resources for their own service needs.

Given these expectations, if you are representing your vendor organization, all your actions, conversations, and presentations should convey this superior quality of thinking and service. In their services role as outlined in this book, CSMs should think hard before they talk. Before explaining to others make sure you can explain to yourself. Poke holes and raise objections privately in your mind. If you cannot answer, consult your colleagues at your own organization, and make sure relevant topics are crystal clear.

Clarity of thought leads to smooth conversations. Employ rational, logical, and critical thinking skills. Use your smartness to create a strong positive influence in your customers' minds. That will help you reap sizeable business benefits in the long run.

KEY TAKEAWAY

Think hard before you talk and act; develop the habit of critical thinking and preparing for whatever action steps you find are necessary

Spoken Language

Verbal eloquence is a key component of the customer success lead role. This individual is the face of the vendor organization and should embody professionalism in all aspects of customer communications, starting with the delivery of the spoken word.

- Use professional English. The corporate world doesn't appreciate slang.
- Form effective and complete sentences. Don't make them too long or too short.
- Speak at a normal pace and pause for breath at logical points of the conversation. Going faster or slower than that may affect the effectiveness of word delivery.
- Don't monopolize the conversation. Let others jump in to add value and perspective.

Digital—Written and Composed Collateral

Quality of the digital communication is important. It has a longer retention period then people's memories. While verbal communications can be forgotten, digital communication is forwarded easily and can be archived for perpetuity. Quality of your documentation prepared and delivered during any of the customer touchpoint phases outlined above will dictate the impression people will have of you, as your written collateral is circulated across the enterprise. This documentation could be manifested as emails, PowerPoint presentations, Word- or PDF-based training materials, Excel-based analysis, or other application-based dashboards or reports. Digital communication has largely two skill components—writing and presentation. While I outline guidance below to improve in both for shorter collateral formats, larger and more time-consuming formats such as books, reports, dashboards, and interfaces should be best handled by specialized resources such as editors and designers.

Writing comes with practice. Before becoming a good writer, be a good reader. Appreciate and enjoy good writing. You will start to emulate, and initially may struggle with words, grammar, and ideas. Share your writing with liberal arts graduates. Incorporate feedback, debate with them and correct your style. The English language provides a fair degree of flexibility, based on geography. Your place of origin will dictate your writing and speaking style. It is however best to tailor your style to your customers' language nuances.

Presentation is equally important if not more compared to the text presented in any digital media. Refer Quality of Collaterals and Talk Tracks section in Chapter 6 for supporting detail. As a skill set, look for continuity, flow, color consistency, ease of message delivery when laying out images on the screen or slides. Spend enough time on presentation layout, review final output or get it reviewed by a third-party, not involved with content preparation, before sending to customer.

Public Speaking

Customer success meetings may have representation from many people from the customer side or just a few. As lead vendor contact, you will need to have the ability to engage with this variable group. Customer success leads that like the bonhomie of small groups may not be comfortable interacting with a larger group. Alternately, good public speakers may get bored with smaller audiences.

If you fall in the former category, look for opportunities to speak at public events. There are groups like Toastmasters and others, as well as continuing education courses in public speaking that might be useful to the reticent or just inexperienced person. It will make you a better speaker, and help you boost credibility further. I suggest use of simple language, free of abbreviations, and composed using commonly known terms, so that your message resonates with a larger audience. Also, when you are preparing to speak publicly, whether a training session or some other speech or lecture, test the pace of word delivery with friends and colleagues, and practice achieving a potent delivery mechanism over time.

For the latter category speakers, they need to understand, that they need to flexible and watch for other challenges that might come their way. Lack of enthusiasm and boredom shows in people's demeanor and could affect customer satisfaction. Customer has paid for your services. It is your responsibility to provide your best.

Effective Trainer

If you bridge the role of CSM and implementation manager (refer to the vendor personae definition in section titled "People" in Chapter 2) you may be called to train customer staff on product usage. CSM is expected to fully understand and be a master of the product that they are enabling at the customer.

Make sure you have clear understanding of your subject matter before you train others. Don't try to learn the product details a day before training and train your audience the next day. You will likely confuse your audience and lose credibility. It is common to see newer staff caught with their pants down when they try to "wing it" through training sessions. Preparation is key before you make a presentation in a training session. The section "Customer Guide" in Chapter 7 provides further information to help prepare for the implementation role. Training is an ongoing activity and starts with the first meeting with customer across all touchpoint phases covered in Part II.

While training, you may encounter a question that you may not have heard or know the answer, despite your knowledge and preparation for a training session. In this case, indicate that you don't have a response right now but will get back to them as soon as possible, and make sure you follow up on your promise with an answer.

Have patience when delivering training. Not everyone grasps concepts in the first hearing. Junior customers or partners in your audience may hold the power now or later to influence your relationship with senior customer executives such as sponsor. Be nice and apply the same relationship management principles outlined throughout this book with the junior staff as well.

EMOTIONAL INTELLIGENCE

Social skills and empathy are crucial skills for developing healthy relationships with customers. They come in handy during tricky situations that invariably come up during customer conversations. I have seen many relationships go sour, despite the best technical resources and vendor solution capabilities, due to a vendor resource's perceived arrogance and behavior during customer interactions. For instance, recent success can adversely affect assigned resources' attitude. During such times, when a vendor and its resources have experienced unprecedented success lately, modesty is a desired trait. To follow are two examples where superior emotional intelligence of a vendor resource helps customer relationships.

Customer Requests and Ideas

Intently listening to customer requests and ideas go a long way in building strong relationships with customers. In most cases, customer requests are valid. Let customers completely deliver their message. For product enhancement requests, do not make and present theories on why something is so and so and should be so and so. Let the product managers and product marketers prepare that talk track. If you bridge these roles, make sure the talk tracks are agreed to by everyone in the vendor leadership team before you relay them to the customer.

Emotionally Charged Situations

Managing a team of passionate and committed team members has its challenges. When everyone is moving in the same direction with a common viewpoint, projects are easy. During differing viewpoints, people with strong opinions can become frustrated when other people don't share them. They may tie the interest of the project to their opinion, and may come out hard on other project stakeholders, both on the customer's and the vendor's side, potentially resulting in hard feelings all around. In such cases, a person who can mediate effectively becomes key to defusing the situation. As a lead CSM on the customer account, this becomes your responsibility.

When faced with such emotionally charged situations, it is best to put your own emotions aside. Request your team members to be calm. Urge them to think, wait for some time before they say anything or send emails when angry.

KEY TAKEAWAYS

Listen intently to customer requests and ideas

Keep your conversations with the customer as positive as possible

Think, wait for some time before you say or send an email when angry

PSYCHOLOGICAL AND MENTAL STRENGTH

Psychological and mental well-being are both crucial to success. Psychological strength refers to the CSM's capacity to control ones' own thoughts, feelings, and behaviors in line with a CSM's objectives as outlined in Part I of this book. Bringing up the courage to speak at a public setting or building consensus are examples where differing aspects of psychological strengths come into play. Mental strength on the other hand helps CSMs deal with stresses, pressures and challenges pertaining to their job. It is important when dealing with people in any situation, but even more so in a customer service position.

Self-Awareness

Every person has some prejudice or bias, whether they will admit to it or not. Most of the time, these biases don't cause any issues in our interpersonal relationships, but in some cases, when a person has grown up with deep rooted prejudices, biases, and insecurities through some incident or the other, these issues can become problematic. In addition, false beliefs, built through some incident or the other, cause potential blind spots and career limiting thinking. This belief is analogous with that of "trained" elephants who when tied with thin rope don't try to break it. They can lift tons of weight and break trees, but they don't try to break the rope, because there is a false belief in their mind that they can't break it.

People that consciously recognize, analyze, and mitigate these elements from their own thinking come out ahead in the long run. They gradually fine-tune their thinking, get feedback, course correct, gain success gradually and become confident over time. For physical attributes, that cannot be changed they accept themselves for the way they are. As CSM, it is important to be in this state sooner than later.

Others around you can quickly see through these psychological gaps if not corrected. When you know what they are, you can make sure they are not exposed during customer and other professional conversations. CSMs with the highest degree of self-awareness are likely to succeed more in this role.

Professional Fit

As a CSM, you need to make sure your own personality traits and skills are aligned with expectations from a CSM role outlined throughout this book. Additionally, it becomes your responsibility to ensure that vendor resources, supporting you in your customer projects, have their skills and personalities aligned with their roles.

Role and skill mismatches tend to cause the same issues highlighted in the previous section—biases, prejudices, false beliefs, and insecurities—in the workplace. The steps outlined in the self-awareness section become crucial to addressing these issues, if they can be corrected with adjustments while staying in the same role.

When there is not an alignment between role expectations and personality, choose the company, department or function that aligns with your skills. If you are not fluent in speaking, writing, or communicating, due to language, cultural or other barriers, move into a manufacturing or programming role where vocal skills may be less relevant. Take roles where you are naturally good and do well in these roles. Play to and impress people with your strengths.

Focus on Strengths Not Weaknesses

Working with strengths is easier than working with weaknesses. While it is important to round out obvious gaps in thinking and execution, excelling requires building on strengths. Athletes, since time immemorial, have chosen and built on their strengths. No one with a handicapped skill that is key to a certain sport can become a world-famous athlete in that sport. For areas that can be improved, take feedback constructively, analyze, understand, and incorporate.

Positive Attitude

Always have and execute your work responsibilities with a positive attitude. Be clear about your priorities and goals. While no work is small or insignificant, choose the ones that are right for your career path. It is best to stay happy on the job and make sure you like what you do. People like to work with happy and enthusiastic people. When your heart is not into it, no matter how much you try, you will not succeed. While you may get by with your supervisors, discerning customers may not appreciate your behavior and negative attitude while interacting with them. In this situation, find a way to get out of the engagement.

KEY TAKEAWAYS

Accept yourself the way you are

Focus on your strengths

Address weaknesses that are addressable

The combination of self-awareness and consistent stream of successes, built on personally experienced failures, will help you achieve both psychological and mental strength

PEOPLE INTERACTION

Building on the emotional, social, psychological, and mental strengths previously described, I outline in this section a few specific approaches to interact with both the customer and vendor personnel involved with your projects.

Dealing with Varied Personality Types

A quick search on the Internet will provide a list of personality types that all of us fall into. We cross over more than one of these types as individuals. Each of these personality types, yearn for something—such as spotlight, friendship, wisdom, experiences, mental stimulation, harmony, expression, leadership opportunities, action, freedom of expression, idealism, certainty, creativity, or old school values.

A good CSM will know how to observe, understand and cater to these personality types among both the customer and vendor personnel involved with the project. The CSM needs to be able to manage the expectations of these different personality types when talking with them individually and facilitate interactions with different personality types when they are working together.

Diplomacy

A good diplomatic persona will help you round out the personality required for this job. I suggest the following diplomatic skills:

- Maintain touch with more than one customer resource
- Don't intimidate anyone with titles, wealth, other college level or professional achievements that could be interpreted as such
- Be humble and helpful
- Tell the truth and keep your message concise (don't provide details that are irrelevant)
- Offer help to customer resources that are coming up to speed
- Build alliances with other vendors and partners serving the same customer
- Watch for competitors and their alliances that could participate in future RFPs (request for proposals) at the customer
- Don't take anything personally and don't carry any grudges.

Coaching Vendor Resources

Set up your associates for success. Let them take charge of appropriate customer conversations. Remember if you lead all conversations, you will never be able to scale. Let associates appear confident in front of customers.

For more details on this topic, refer to Chapter 13, titled "Supervising and Managing Vendor Resources." Your supervisors and you will need to follow the principles outlined there to grow your organization.

Friendship

Friendships are built with natural chemistries and honest intent. Pretense and charades don't help and are usually a waste of time. Make long term friendships with your points of contact. When they leave their firms and join others, they will likely carry your business with you. In fact, make friends everywhere you go—airports, flights, restaurants, health clubs—whenever possible. Don't aggressively reach out but stay accessible. Such friendships help when relationships take a turn for the worse in adverse scenarios.

On the flip side, when you encounter a bump in your relationship, due to a loss or misunderstanding, absorb the loss and give the other person the benefit of doubt. In the CSM role, consider yourself as an investor who will reap rewards from the customer relationship in the longer run. Short term losses and expenses, such as implementation rework, will be covered by future windfalls such as via cross-sell, upsell, renewals, and new license opportunities. Reach out to your supervisor when you encounter such situations and make a business case for continued investment.

If the relationship goes sour or the customer contact has concerns with your style, it is better to hand the account to someone else on your team. There is a fine line between negotiating a bump in the road with a customer (which can be overcome) and admitting there is a problem there that is better solved by someone else. If you are having a relational conflict with a customer or someone on your team, however, it might be best to clear the air with your supervisor about the situation.

Lastly, there are situations when vendors attempt to experiment with customer messaging related to product roadmap, estimates, expenses, and expectations from customer—that may turn out to be unacceptable to customers. There are other cases, where CSMs are overloaded with work and are unable to cope up with supervisor demands. Attempts to juggle multiple tasks at once could result in dropped balls adversely affecting the health of the project. The combination of unacceptable messaging and dropped balls from the CSM, in addition to potential CSM gaps, could affect customer's relationship with the CSM. In such situations, supervisors need to understand root causes to avoid the same result with the replacement CSM on the customer's project.

12

CUSTOMER MEETINGS

THE ABILITY TO CHAIR MEETINGS with big and small audiences is a crucial skill set for the customer success manager. Successful meeting outcomes are dependent on basic principles, adherence to which can help the customer success individual rise in his or her career. Aligning agenda of all relevant stakeholders and managing it through completion is essentially the key outcome of all customer meetings. I categorize all sections in this chapter into planning, execution, etiquette, travel, and telecommute technology groups.

PLANNING

Planning section covers all considerations before a meeting starts. This includes identifying appropriate participants, checking availability, sending invites, planning agenda and spending reasonable time before the call to think through meeting outcomes.

Number of Customer Meetings and Participants

Time management and relationship development suggestions may seem to conflict with each other. Latter takes time and cannot be rushed. There is a healthy balance that need to be maintained depending on the situation. The "Customer Touchpoint Frequency" section in Chapter 7 covers meeting suggestions and supported frequency. Make sure each touchpoint is meaningful and informative. From time efficiency standpoint, before you call a meeting, ask yourself if it is necessary.

At the same time, maximize time with as many customer contacts from bonding and business development standpoint. For meetings where vendor is presenting results from a key milestone or with business development intent, I recommend inviting a larger customer group to attend meetings. Your customer contact may not make it happen, but there is nothing wrong in asking for more customer side people's participation. You want to build multiple relationships and not depend on just one or two individuals to carry the customer relationship. There is typically a higher degree of churn in senior level positions on customer side. Backup relationships, without antagonizing the main customer contact, are strongly recommended for the continued health of customer vendor relationship.

I also recommend representation by more than one person from vendor side in all customer meetings or recording of all customer meetings. This helps during meeting debriefs, training and course corrections post meetings.

Value participants time and invite them only when necessary. Let customer contact forward invites to their side of participant list. At large organizations, this protocol is more relevant. After the first few meetings, customer contact may allow you to send the invites directly.

KEY TAKEAWAYS

Maximize your time with customer contacts from bonding standpoint, while maintaining efficiency in managing the relationship and implementations

Interact with multiple contacts on customer side to avoid relationship disruptions due to attrition

Always have more than one vendor person attend meetings with customers

Coordinating Meeting Times

While this step may look straightforward, mismanagement can cause aggravation and embarrassment. Make sure you look at your own calendar every day, before and after work to get a handle on existing meetings and available times for other meetings. Establish a daily routine and accordingly identify times where the likelihood of conflicts on your calendar are less. Ask yourself these questions before you schedule calls: "Are you free from personal calls?" or "Does your manager leave you alone at that time?" You get the idea. If there are colleagues accompanying you for customer meetings, ensure you get buy in from them as well.

Once the vendor side times are nailed down, reach out to the customer with available time slots. Keep in mind time zone differences for remote meeting participants. Align and send out invites accordingly.

KEY TAKEAWAY

Identify a time that is least likely to run into a conflict before reaching out to the customer

Calendar Invites

Given the multi-oriented nature of both customer contact and customer-facing roles, most audience members depend on the calendar invite to get meeting details before the meeting. Before sending out the calendar invite, ensure you have captured directly in the invite the agenda, web meeting details with dial in information, web sharing links, onsite addresses, and directions as appropriate, and reference attachments or links. I will cover email contents later in the book. For now, suffice it to say, large email and calendar attachments should generally be avoided. For reoccurring meetings, ensure they are agreed to ahead of time before you block people's calendars.

Most people on the receiving end don't appreciate when their calendars are blocked without permission. They will likely show their unhappiness or won't show up for the meeting. Either way the exercise is not worth it, although it is still being pursued by aggressive sales personnel and their sales managers.

KEY TAKEAWAYS

Most people don't appreciate when their calendars are blocked without permission

Capture relevant details and meeting context in the calendar invite

Meeting Agenda

Every meeting should have an agenda: always publish agenda before every meeting and end with an agenda for the next meeting if a subsequent meeting is necessary.

Inventory the full list of topics and prioritize them starting with the most important one. Contentious topics should generally be left to the end, so that they can picked up after gaining momentum on the other ones, and after a positive tone is established earlier. Share the agenda with the participants ahead of time, so that everyone is prepared before the meeting.

Try to do more with less. Productive meetings are appreciated. When you cover a lot demonstrably, people look at you as an efficient resource. If you realize that meetings consistently run out of time, adjust your agenda list or meeting time so that there is always a right balance. If you manage customer's time well, you will invariably become their go to person for future needs.

I generally don't recommend allotting time per agenda item ahead of the meeting. It is usually a difficult, unnecessary and pointless exercise. At best, give people a general idea so that they know that enough representation will be provided to appropriate topics.

KEY TAKEAWAYS

Every meeting should have an agenda

Manage your customer's time well

Stick with the agenda but don't be completely rigid

Rescheduling

It is not unrealistic to get rescheduling requests from the customer, your own team members or even from yourself, if personal or other professional conflicts come up. Slip ups occur too, when meetings run over, when you or others lose track of time, or when simply you or others are unaware of conflicts. Most people in the workforce understand that such situations do come up. While inconvenient, most people entertain reschedule requests, if they don't become a reoccurring theme.

Making sure both parties and participants understand and agree to guidelines concerning rescheduling protocol is beneficial from the start. During the first conversation with the customer, say during implementation kickoff, I suggest you bond with the customer and set expectations about such situations. Start on the right side of the customer with a good first impression. Look for similarities in each other's background—such as college, sport, hobby, or geography. It is never a good idea to reschedule the very first meeting since that may not set a good first impression. Once you build a good rapport with the customer and participants, it will be much easier to get alternate meeting times during conflicts.

With a regular habit of checking and rechecking your calendar, your calendar will stay up-to-date. CSMs who wear multiple hats or involved in multiple projects may get called into meetings at short notice. Alternately your key participant may get pulled into conflicting time slot tasks and meetings. Make it a priority to guard your meeting invites and minimize disruptions during the meeting times.

KEY TAKEAWAY

Manage your calendar well and track your time during meetings to avoid reschedule situations

Preparation and Alertness Before Meeting

As with coordinating meetings, check your calendar at the end and in the beginning of every day, to best prepare for your meetings. Review upcoming calendar invites and ascertain inclusion of elements discussed in meetings held till date. Refer to notes from previous meetings. Follow up on action items identified till date with respective owners. Ensure you take care of your own action items committed for completion prior to the call.

For meetings that were scheduled way ahead of time with no recent touchpoints, reach out to participants to confirm if they can still join.

Always think through and visualize the upcoming conversation flow, meeting tone, potential issues, and disputes. A certain amount of nervousness before every meeting is a good sign. It shows that you are not complacent and not taking everything for granted.

KEY TAKEAWAYS

Check your calendar periodically for upcoming meetings

Call ahead to confirm participation by attendees

Think through, visualize the upcoming conversation flow, and plan accordingly

EXECUTION

Smooth meetings leave a good taste. Rocky conversations can have disastrous consequences. The result of most meetings can be positively influenced, with streamlined execution and via adherence to the principles shared in this book.

In this section, I cover considerations that come into play while the meeting is in progress from start to end.

Time Management

Start your meetings on time and attempt to end on time or early. Participants appreciate when they get back time to breathe before their next meeting or task. Top of the hour and bottom of the hour terms are used commonly to communicate stipulated meeting end times. The "top of the hour" refers to, for example, 3 p.m., while the "bottom of the hour" would refer to 3:30 p.m. Make sure you are clear about the time of a meeting's beginning and end.

Follow the agenda and urge participants to stick with the plan. Setup separate meetings for sequential topics that originate from the meeting. However, if an interesting, creative aspect is introduced, don't interrupt. Let the idea emerge. If the conversation takes long, capture notes, setup and build on it in a separate meeting. If meetings catch momentum and if everyone is engaged, adjust plans to go beyond the stipulated end time.

However, extending meetings is usually difficult. People are often just booked. Identify a logical stopping point in the conversation, and then suggest a short follow-up meeting, if possible, to cover the topics that were not discussed, or consider continuing the discussion online through email or another mode of communication. In general, always anticipate the nature of the conversation and estimate more time than needed. Periodically let people know the time left before meeting is about to end.

Give maximum talking time to the customer while controlling the conversation and running the meeting effectively and efficiently. Let the client speak if there is meaningful extraction of data. If something is not clear, wait till the customer finishes to avoid breaking their train of thought. Make sure your questions and clarification requests are insightful.

For online meetings, if there is a technology connectivity hiccup, or other issues in any one or more participant lines, silence or hold music can be awkward. Let the meeting leader deal with it. Wait for 30 seconds or longer, if still no response or if you are the meeting leader, acknowledge the issue and reschedule the meeting.

KEY TAKEAWAYS

Follow the agenda and urge participants to stick with the plan

Anticipate issues and plan accordingly

If an interesting thought comes up and meetings run over, don't interrupt, check with everyone, and extend the meeting accordingly

Participant Engagement

This section may seem to contradict with the previous one. While time management is important, CSM should use every opportunity to bond with their customers. I lay out balancing considerations so that you get the full perspective side by side.

When you conduct meetings, in most cases stick with the agenda but don't be completely rigid. There should always be scope for airing free format ideas and to allow customer side audience to get a sense of ownership and be part of the project. People like to talk and feel important. Every conversation may not be about work alone. Let the meetings have an element of human touch. Purely technical and serious conversations can feel stressful and inadvertently affect productivity and enthusiasm to be part of these meetings.

Start your meetings with light pleasantries, check the mood and get on with it. In most cases people want to cut to the chase. Watch for customers that have a talkative personality. Remember you need to manage your own time and be accountable for the results. The same customer who seemingly killed time, will seek answers for project delays and sloppy error prone implementations.

As you get to know clients over time, you find out what things they like to talk about. Stay attuned to customers' personal interests and bond with small talk while watching time. During meetings, there should be limited time for personal interests, hobbies, vacations, and even sports. These are good for bonding purposes but that is about it. Don't immerse yourself in these topics.

Keep your and other's personal stories—good or bad—private. Keep your issues and gripes to yourself. Likewise attempt to control your own supporting vendor resources' personal concerns during professional settings.

Finally, no one is interested in hearing about your vacation stories—good or bad. While your dear friends may indulge you, your customers may not.

KEY TAKEAWAYS

There is limited time for sports and vacation conversations

Keep your eye on project execution tasks; that above all takes precedence

Notes

People, especially in a professional setting, remember what they said and expect others to remember too. Customers are not forgiving when they are asked to repeat things, especially in the first one or two meeting sessions.

It is the responsibility of the vendor's resources to take notes, send to everyone's attention after the meeting and to refer to them before the next meeting.

Note taking is an important skill for the customer success manager. While there are web meeting recording and transcription facilities, there is no automated solution that can distill the meeting notes into clear summaries and action items. If meetings depend on such recorded information for notes, someone must wait for the recording or transcription, extract out the summary and action items and send them after the meeting. This could be a time-consuming task. Further, useful items that are not obvious from a transcript may be lost if not recorded in notes.

CSMs wear multiple hats and deal daily with customers one after another and are pressed for time. I recommend that they get into the habit of capturing notes, summaries and action items real time in logical format during the call. Web meetings allow sharing of participant's screens, so other participants can read captured notes as they are captured during the meeting, further confirming accuracy and boosting transparency. After some minor edits, these notes can be sent out right after the call, when the memory is fresh, and details can be retained. If this effort is held up for the end of the day or later in the week, the chances of mistyping exact notes get higher.

I usually recommend clearing your plate right away so that you are free to move on to other responsibilities. In this case, emailing notes right away after the meeting will help you keep everyone in the loop constantly and help you and others refer to the notes immediately and before the next meeting. You will always be on top of things and will be able to execute your projects effectively.

Confirm distribution list with the customer, before you broadcast them to customer side audience. Many customer contacts reserve the right to manage exposure to customer side resources.

KEY TAKEAWAYS

Capturing notes is not an option

Take notes, as conversations occur,
in front of participants, so that there is
clear line of understanding and ownership of tasks

Recording Conversations

I suggest you record all customer-facing sessions. Before you record, get permission from customer-side participants. Use web meeting services that auto-transcribe recordings and those that provide unlimited recording space. Running out of space can be a hindrance in the middle of the day, when you have important customer meetings lined up.

Check with your management about delete-recording policies. Some leaders never want to delete anything and like to hoard data that go back years. Others are realistic and only selectively retain data. I recommend the latter, since it is easier to search and retrieve this information when needed. Imagine going through countless hours of recording time from multiple years of recordings! In today's fast-paced world, would you want to pore through recordings from previous years? If for training, wouldn't you want to depend more on up-to-date training material that is marked as such. Training specific recordings should be inventoried in your document management system and not left on the web meeting vendor's storage space. Recordings are typically used to refer to recent conversations to prepare for future conversations.

KEY TAKEAWAYS

Record customer conversations after taking permission

Transfer important recordings to your document management
systems and tag them with self-explanatory identifiers

Action Items

Always end your meetings with an action plan, unless the meeting agenda is purely status update. In the case of latter, email of meeting notes alone may suffice. Other than these special situations, most meetings should be action oriented. That will ensure progressive completion of project plan activities.

Avoid assigning work to your customer contacts, unless it is a large project and requires extensive collaboration with the customer, as in the case of system integration demands that require deeper involvement of respective customer personnel. The vendor should attempt to address most action items arising out of customer meetings. This approach will ensure the fastest path to implementation and deployment. As covered in the "Customer Motivation" section in Chapter 7, for customer-assigned action items, be polite. Don't push. Make do with what you have and iterate after you have finally managed to enthusiastically engage the customer.

Get into the habit of clearing your plate during and after every meeting. Prepare a list of tasks and assignments and send them with notes. Address all your items that are quick wins. For time-consuming ones, block your own calendar right away to work on your own tasks.

KEY TAKEAWAYS

Meetings should be action oriented

Vendors should pick up most, if not all, of the workload for fastest path to execution

ETIQUETTE

In this section, I cover protocols and expectations from all meeting participants to maintain decorum and to respect everyone's time and views.

Participant Expectations

It is important to establish conversation control on both sides - customer and vendor—when multiple participants from each side are involved in the conversation. Customer contact and CSM should drive the conversations respectively from their sides. Each side—customer and vendor—should use only one spokesperson. Have one person represent the full group from respective sides. Typically, a CSM represents all vendor resources and a customer project manager represents customer resources. As CSM, discuss talk tracks with vendor resources ahead of time. Vendor resources should then be assigned roles and specific talk tracks for delivery.

Sometimes vendors want to show strength via numbers and ask many people from the vendor side to be present. Not all these people should speak after brief introductions at the beginning of the call or meeting. As facilitator, watch for team members who could speak out of turn and blurt "unofficial" not approved points of view. Non-active participant vendor resources should be advised to pay attention even if the message (to be conveyed by other vendor resources) has been heard before. Non-leading participants should take ample notes and send them to the official note taker for aggregation. They need to speak only when asked and should stay to the point in message delivery. Do not share spur of the moment thinking. Better to stay silent than to attempt pulling back unapproved, in appropriate commentary after it is delivered. As a rule, "if in doubt, don't say anything." Let experienced and informed associates handle the conversations.

KEY TAKEAWAYS

Speak in one voice

Allow non leading participants to speak only when asked

Deliver preapproved talk tracks only

Apologizing

Most expect strong leaders to be correct more often than wrong. The need for situations where one needs to apologize should only come about in rare situations. Preparation and forethought are key to avoiding these situations. Demonstrate strength, discipline, and consistent follow through. Need to apologize may not arise.

For mistakes and errors in judgement, it is perfectly okay to apologize, course correct, and move on. Humility is appreciated and apologizing does reflect that to some extent. When mistakes occur, people expect you to apologize, defuse the situation, and move on.

KEY TAKEAWAYS

Prepare, so that you don't have to apologize

Apologize, for genuine mistakes from you or your team. People will appreciate

Showing up Early

Barring unusual circumstances, never be late for customer meetings. For onsite meetings, plan to reach the meeting location about 15 to 30 minutes early. Know the address, location, and directions well ahead of time. If need be, drive the night before if the place is unfamiliar. Plan to book your hotel next to the client location to save travel time and to avoid traffic right before meeting time.

For web meetings, plan to dial in 2 to 5 minutes before the meeting. If it is a new web meeting solution, click on the link ahead of time so that the required web plugins are installed and ready to go. Be respectful of others' time. If you are the meeting owner, let people know ahead of time about this protocol.

For online meetings, vendor and customer executives are typically let off the hook as they struggle through web meeting plugin setup while the meeting is in progress. Don't call them out. People in these roles juggle a lot and should be afforded some slack. Try to anticipate this situation and plan accordingly.

KEY TAKEAWAYS

Plan to dial in early for web meetings and show up early for onsite meetings

Test the web meeting tools and know your meeting location ahead of time

No Question Is Stupid—But Should We Ask

Many instructors and meeting coordinators start with the statement "no question is stupid, feel free to ask any question." As an audience member I have exchanged glances with fellow mates, with the unsaid expression "now that was really stupid," OR "didn't we go over this already."

Before you ask any question in public, make sure you ask that question to yourself and see if you can answer yourself with critical thinking. If you missed a certain section, reach out to your colleagues in private. Be respectful of other's time and hold that question till then. The quality of your questions will affect the impression you leave on others. So, think hard before you ask.

Pay attention during customer conversations, in class or any public classroom or panel session even if you are not actively participating. It is best not to multitask. If you need to multitask and are still requested on the call, mention ahead of time to the meeting coordinator that you are working on something else, and need to be prompted to get back in the conversation.

KEY TAKEAWAYS

Attempt to answer your question yourself before you ask in public

Quality of your questions will affect the impression you leave on others

Pay attention during meetings even if you are not leading the conversation

We Just Covered It

Many titled executives and managers when they show up late to meetings and training sessions, assume it is okay to make the meeting leader or instructor repeat the points that they missed. Worse, they go in and out of sessions, repeating the same behavior again and again.

I recommend instructors correct such behaviors through subtle hints or in tactful private one on one conversations with these individuals. Customers don't appreciate when this same behavior is reflected in customer-facing meetings.

KEY TAKEAWAY

Don't encourage interrupting behavior of senior executives during meetings

Ambush

The same senior executives have the habit of popping into meetings midway and hijacking the conversation either into a rat hole or a completely off topic discussion.

These behaviors are wrong for multiple reasons. It is disrespectful to the person who set up the meeting and to the audience members whose expectations now are misaligned. Such senior personae tend to lose credibility and limit their career growth through these actions.

If you are an executive, don't fall into this trap. Have confidence in your customer success staff and associates. If you send your staff to these meetings, train them, and convey your perspectives ahead of the meeting. If the staff member is new, or not trained, set expectations with the audience ahead of time. With this preparation, your associates will be more than able to either disseminate or gather the appropriate information based on the nature of the meeting or session.

As a customer success manager, if you are reporting to such an executive, don't feel apologetic and assume that you did something wrong. Be diplomatic and get control back to run the agenda as socialized earlier. In such situations, I politely point out that we are going off topic to the executive. Most people understand and take the conversation offline after the meeting.

KEY TAKEAWAYS

Watch for executives who hijack your meetings

Executives should have confidence in their staff leading customer conversations

Customer success staff should be trained and equipped to handle customer success conversations

TRAVEL AND TELECOMMUTE TECHNOLOGY

In this section, I cover elements that come into play while meeting customers in person or virtually using audio visual enabled teleconferencing technologies.

First Impressions

A healthy relationship starts with a favorable first impression. Many of the points explained in this book, such as preparation, communication, and dress code, will help you establish a strong first impression, and then carry that favorable relationship forward. Depending on your skill set and job profile, few or all these points will be crucial in getting on the right side of the customer.

For instance, a nontechnical resource may need to focus on dress code and quality of speech. Alternately, if you are onsite for technical hands-on or advisory work, make sure your tools and technical word tracks are in order. Dazzle them the very first time with your knowledge.

Shaky starts usually lead to rough conversations later down the line. Prepare, prepare, and prepare before your first meeting to avoid such situations.

Calling on Customers During Onsite Travel

If you plan to travel for business, especially large cities, meet as many customers as possible in that area. You will likely have multiple clients in a concentrated area. Call them in advance, and check schedules. They will meet you, if they like you and find purpose. Prepare convincing talk tracks, set, and circulate the agenda ahead of meetings. No one likes to meet for the sake of meeting. Time is precious, value their time and yours. Make those meetings action oriented, and act on the identified action items. Otherwise, the chances of meeting with them again will be limited.

KEY TAKEAWAYS

Make the most of your travel when visiting major cities by meeting multiple customer contacts

Have a purpose, make the customers' time worthwhile and act on the identified action items

Dress Code

Pay attention to your business attire for onsite presence. Check ahead of time if you need business formal or business casual clothing. Silicon Valley is generally laid back and typically follows the latter approach for professional settings. With that said, it is better to be over dressed as opposed to under dressed when in doubt.

When working and dialing into web meetings from home, plan to wear business casual clothing and be well groomed during work hours. Increasingly, web meetings auto-activate video conferencing and you may project less than ideal video recording of yourself inadvertently.

KEY TAKEAWAYS

It is better to be over dressed as opposed to under dressed when in doubt

While working from home, wear business casual and sit in an office setup for web meetings

Travel Considerations

During customer visits, you will likely be at airports, restaurants, coffee shops, taxis, and numerous other similar places where you usually don't go. When an activity is not done regularly, the chances of you forgetting something is much higher. You may leave your laptop, bag, or wallet behind, resulting in not only financial hardship and inconvenience, but also embarrassment in front of your customers and colleagues. Checking and cross-checking habit will consistently come to your aid if you can adopt it. Look behind and scan the area before you stand, exit, step out, or move from one place to another.

KEY TAKEAWAY

Check and double check for your belongings
before you stand, exit, step out,
or move from one place to another

Video Conferencing

Company offices are gradually augmented with video conferencing facilities. In most cases the same meeting protocols as relevant for onsite meetings apply. In addition, pay attention to the location of the cameras and voice recording devices. The technology setup is many a times not as seamless as you would expect for a natural in person conversation.

You may be expected to speak closer to the audio recorder and face the camera directly. Cameras should be placed close to the monitor so that you can see the remote location participants and speak to them in the same direction.

Be mindful of the environment around you when you are on a video conference call. Flipping pages of paper, typing on a keyboard, and even side conversations among non-participants will create sounds that will be captured immediately and cause interruption during the meeting. If you are using a speakerphone, using the mute button when you are not speaking can help to minimize these issues.

13

SUPERVISING AND MANAGING VENDOR RESOURCES

CONTINUOUS EXECUTIVE LEVEL INVOLVEMENT OF a vendor's senior management during all phases as outlined in Part II is very important. I covered customer end reviews and audit in Part II. The same principles apply for vendor side supervision and review too, with heightened focus on people, process, and training development. Vendor's senior management should proactively provide ongoing guidance to on-ground staff and course correct before the damage is irreparable. In this chapter, I outline considerations for supervisors who supervise CSMs. I refer to the body of supervisors as vendor's senior management and call out the supervisor role explicitly when I address them in this chapter.

Based on the scale of the phases outlined in Part II, senior management should assign resources based on their experience, domain expertise, and personality traits. Fortune 1000 accounts, for instance, that hold a lot of potential, even if small in the beginning, should be considered sensitive accounts and should have senior most involvement.

Building on the concepts laid out in Part I of this book, all customer projects should have defined success metrics that are periodically measured and monitored by vendor executives. Deviances should be acted on immediately.

Senior management at vendor side should have the desired people management skills. They should be good listeners, should be passionate about the growth of their staff's careers, and should be their guide on both professional and personal fronts. When ground staff look up to their management with inspiration and awe, they (staff) will automatically provide years of loyalty at their jobs.

Lastly, the CSM and all other vendor roles should be staffed adequately. Employee burnout is a serious risk and can damage the financial health of the vendor organization. Employees' physical and mental health is inextricably tied to their employer's bottom-line health. Senior management should accordingly distribute the customer accounts to their staff keeping in mind on-ground staff's bandwidth constraints.

High-Level Challenges

Vendors face growing pains when they sign up significant number of customers with a limited number of vendor resources to back customer implementations. New resources are hired who need to be trained on the vendor's technology or require customer success training if brought in from other roles. Unexpected attrition at the vendor could cause similar bandwidth constraints and knowledge transfer challenges. The fast-paced nature of the CSM job, alongside the need to track and record each interaction across all their customers, makes it inherently difficult to provide desired level of visibility and scrutiny. Lastly, every product vendor's focus is on license revenue, new accounts, and minimization of implementation costs. Accordingly, CSMs are invariably asked to handle many accounts, and take on more responsibilities, leaving less time for documentation and supervisor reporting.

Next, I touch on a few undesired outcomes, resulting from such situations, to lay the groundwork for the rest of the chapter.

1. Difficulty in sharing loose uncollated notes and collaterals with senior management

2. Vendor organization's resources aligned more with customer wins compromising retention

3. Customer relationships irreversibly torn affecting contract renewals
4. Lack of visibility of souring relationships till it is too late
5. Investor perception of product usability and adoption much different from reality
6. Investor sanctioned audits and supervision are not frequent enough to provide real time and accurate picture of the health of their investments

COACHING

The key responsibility of every supervisor should be to offer help and coaching. For every sensitive project and customer, supervisors should be always current on project risk status and ask for explanations from CSMs as appropriate. Supervisors need to coach CSM with the right talk tracks, get budget to execute vendor side remediation measures or work with customer leadership to make a business case for them to implement required measures. Supervisors should ensure sensitive conversations and relationships are handled carefully by sharp and patient staff.

At risk customer relationships are difficult to revive. Supervisors are best positioned to handle such situations, keeping the stress away from the assigned CSM. Once a customer loses interest in a project, nothing much can be done. Even so, relationship exits are not always abrupt. Customer service dialog may continue to stay open, with both parties touching base periodically, until the subscription period runs out. Vendors may continue to solicit old accounts, although halfheartedly, till emails and voicemails eventually stop receiving replies. In such cases, when interest begins to lag, supervisors should choose their battles wisely and limit CSM's time on follow ups.

URGE TO CONTROL

Supervisors should empower their associates and resist controlling CSM actions, including but not limited to talk tracks, emails, and presentations. When supervisors pursue a risk averse approach or are unsure of their associates' ability to lead customer conversations, they tend to spend disproportionate time reviewing CSM work.

This results in a constant look over the shoulder syndrome by the customer success resource, and dilutes their confidence, making them less effective. At small vendor organizations, looking over one's shoulder every time, and cross-checking with the supervisor before and after every customer conversation, may slow a CSM's pace unproductively.

Gradual success in managing outcomes raise a CSM's own and a supervisor's confidence. Supervisors should enable their CSMs to build a stream of successes while following supervisor's constant monitoring. As CSMs achieve success, supervisors can establish clear boundaries of the type of decisions CSMs can take vs. consulting with supervisor.

Supervisors should let their associates refine their own techniques and conversation style while staying in line with company policies and procedures. As covered in the "Ambush" section in Chapter 12, titled "Customer Meetings," they should have confidence in their customer success staff and associates.

Before supervisors send their staff to handle customer relationships, they need to train their staff, and convey employing organization's perspectives ahead of transferring this responsibility. If the staff member is new, or not trained, supervisors need to set staff-in-training expectations with the customer audience ahead of time. With this preparation and level setting, CSMs will be more than able to either disseminate or gather the appropriate information based on the nature of the meeting or session.

EMPLOYEE ENGAGEMENT

Given the heightened attention for customer acquisition, supervisors can get stressed when their staff makes inadvertent mistakes or are generally unable to manage projects due to skill limitations or external factors beyond their staff's control. It is important to remember in such situations, that it is easier to acquire customers by vendor, compared to finding and retaining skilled engaged staff. Building a strong CSM team is more important, and therefore supervisors should pay special attention to retaining and training their staff.

When customer relationships go sour, supervisors should root cause reasons, which could be product, vendor personnel, customer's unique situation and or external factors such as regulatory intervention. If supervised staff is responsible, drill down further to see if they need skills, are not motivated or are not aligned personality wise with the desired roles and expectations. For inadvertent mistakes it is best to excuse them. Provide guidance, let go and monitor behavior till it is corrected. Don't belabor the point or berate staff. Write off losses and move on. Unless the employee is sloppy or disinterested, give them a chance, and train them.

As a supervisor, you will be a winner in the long run. These same individuals will turn out to be loyal resources, and key pillars of your company and group's future growth.

14

CSM OPERATIONS

IN THIS CHAPTER, I RESUME focus on activities performed by CSMs to work with their supervisors and peers. The world is not perfect. CSMs may get supervised by inexperienced supervisors and CSMs should delicately handle the supervisor relationship as supervisors settle into their roles. I provide guidance to address such supervisory gaps in this section. This chapter has an operational focus and covers specific actions that CSMs should and should not do to rise in their careers.

SUCCESS METRIC REPORTING (TO VENDOR STAKEHOLDERS)

Reporting is an essential component of CSM's responsibilities to provide adequate visibility to supervisors and other stakeholders on the vendor side. I covered monitoring tools and aids required to measure success early and throughout this book. A vendor's own cloud or on-premise platform, along with third-party systems integrated with the vendor's platform provide information on usage and realized metrics. Deployed survey responses collect qualitative feedback from end users using or trying to use the system. Contract collaterals, meeting notes provide desired goals and ongoing status of the project. All these add an element of monitoring and accountability to the process. Given the magnitude of this information a customer success software solution helps streamline this data set.

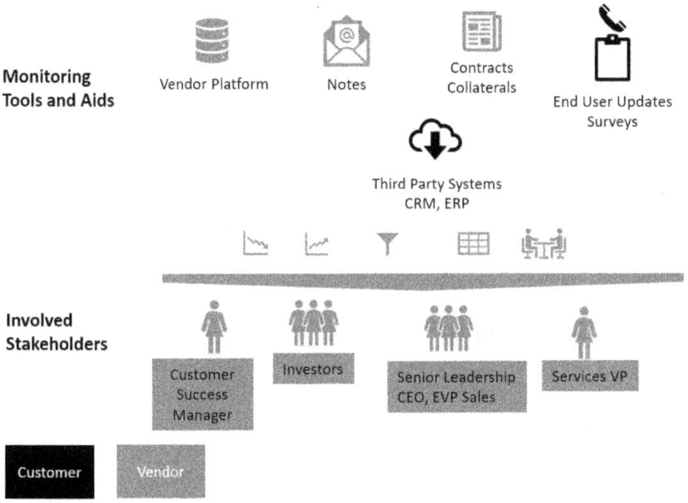

Figure14.1: Success Metric Reporting—Resources and Stakeholders

Vendor resources led by CSM work with customer end personnel to collect relevant data, execute, and support the activities in the following table.

ACTIVITY:
Data Collection and Report Development

Description: CSM collects inputs from end users, internal and third-party systems, prepares reports and dashboards for respective stakeholders.

ACTIVITY:
Senior Management Review of Collaterals

Description: Review content prepared for customer meetings by vendor resources, meeting notes, and success metrics.

ACTIVITY:
Investor (of Vendor) Review

Description: Review customer success metrics from each of their investment portfolio companies. Each vendor from this portfolio may be required to send metrics across all their respective customers to their investor group.

INTERNAL REPORTING

As a CSM handling multiple customer relationships, you may be required to send weekly reports to your supervisors. I have included a few components of this report in the "Customer Success Report Format" section of the Appendices. The account characteristics in the format will help you and your team sort, filter, and prioritize accounts.

Report preparation can be time intensive if you don't always get into the habit of keeping this report updated daily and weekly. As you finish meetings, document summary updates for every key conversation held with the customers. Follow the suggestions outlined in the Chapter 12, titled "Customer Meetings." Record dates of last meeting and upcoming meeting dates. I suggest you review all active accounts weekly. This cadence will not only help your manager, but also make sure you do not miss out on any critical tasks assigned to any member of your team, including yourself.

Depending on your working style and customer success update meeting time, finish the report and send it on a fixed day of the week, every week. Friday's could work best if your manager likes to review such reports over weekends. Many people tend to work long hours on Fridays to clear their plates, so that nothing is left for the weekend. Others prefer to wrap up Friday's activities early and pick up over the weekend or early next week.

Since this documentation triggers preparation, execution and planning for multiple leftover tasks, plan to keep enough hours for this work and start early so that you don't have to work late in the evenings or weekends and risk burnout, exhaustion, and a disruption in your life balance.

Don't make it a habit of working on weekends. Keep weekend work very infrequent and limited to light management update calls.

Customer Success Update Meeting

Request your audience to read delivered reports ahead of time so that you limit your time on these calls. Don't let the meeting stretch on for more than 30 to 60 minutes. Inexperienced supervisors are notorious time eaters. Watch for such behaviors. One can tactfully try to redirect the conversation, and if it is a persistent problem, discuss it diplomatically offline. If there is an understanding, and the supervisor tends to wander into the wilderness again, a quick text reminder can help. Don't allow the report format to change every week. Once there is agreement on the format in the beginning, collect feedback regularly but allow updates to the report format infrequently. Otherwise, you will spend a lot of time on just reporting effort as opposed to doing actual customer success work.

REQUESTS SENT TO INTERNAL RESOURCES

Collaboration is crucial to supporting interdependent company operations. Everyone in the company is busy. So be patient when requests sent to internal resources are not fulfilled.

Further, it is easy to forget, especially if it is a small company, division, or a part-time group, and everyone is running at a million miles per hour. Don't expect someone to execute after the first request. Reach out after some time, based on the pattern observed with that group. If need be, put meetings on their calendars to follow up.

WORKING WITH INEXPERIENCED SUPERVISORS

The world is imperfect for multiple reasons. Inexperienced personnel are asked to lead divisions. Many smooth talk their way to the top but when they get there, they either wing it or simply act as messengers to route instructions top down. They make carte blanche statements on customer related topics without much appreciation of ground reality.

Irrespectively, they will expect you to handle the details and variations when interacting with your customers. Be careful of following their advice. If you follow them to the word, and still fail, they will likely still hold you accountable. Remember it is your relationship. If for any reason, it is affected, your head is on the line.

Instead of your managers, your coworkers may be better than the appointed leaders for advice. They appreciate ground reality and have a better idea of handling these situations, given their firsthand experience with such situations.

FEEDBACK LOOP IN MATURE ORGANIZATIONS

Mature organizations are careful about who they promote, and leadership usually emerges from the trenches. Your manager would likely have faced your challenges before you do. Depending on the size of the customer, loss of even one customer account could have serious consequences to the organization and you. In such cases, if in doubt, consult your manager one on one. Let the person make the call, putting the responsibility of the decision on him or her. At mature organizations, this approach works best and is desired.

As boots on the ground, it is your job to make sure you pass through all relevant information and submit your suggestions for potential course of action.

CSM JOB ACCEPTANCE AND UNDERSTANDING

Understand the landscape before you take on customer success roles. Discuss with your hiring manager, modes of operation, team setup, product maturity and customer retention rates. Products that have not matured or have poor retention rates even after being around for certain years should be approached with caution. Ask for accounts that have renewed after one, two and three years.

If renewals are less than 40 percent after the first year, chances of your survival in the company are going to be very less. Without a substantial equity stake that is vested immediately, without a substantial source of investment, and without a clear game plan to turn around the situation, think through the situation, consult with your manager or trusted colleagues with experience, and consider other opportunities if it does not look like you have a good fit.

Set expectations at time of employment. Billable utilization of one's own hours, implementation health, successful adoption, and license renewal demands can get excessive. Establish realistic key process indicators especially when considering roles at startups.

PROFESSIONAL GROWTH SUGGESTIONS

This section is designed to help CSMs avoid pitfalls and pursue desired traits from a professional development standpoint. A short sampling of representative considerations will help CSMs watch for seemingly insignificant actions that could become career limiting steps. On the other hand, positive moves outlined here will be recognized, appreciated, and help you execute your role efficiently and effectively. To set expectations for my readers, I emphasize that this is very short list. It is included here for general awareness and to convey the point that small actions can have significant both positive and negative impact.

Elevator Etiquette

It feels natural to start a conversation with fellow colleagues or clients on a long elevator ride. Whatever you do, stay away from confidential topics. Elevators are likely shared by other tenants in the building who could be competitors or simply are not interested in listening into that conversation. Respect their privacy while protecting your intellectual property.

More specifically, never talk about a customer project or worse, cover its sensitive details in an elevator. It can get embarrassing, if your company

CEO or executive and a competitor or customer contact happen to be in the elevator at that time.

Moonlighting

A second job or parallel business initiative cannot conflict with your position in the organization and your employment agreement. Look for a company policy before you pursue a parallel opportunity. Irrespectively, if you like to pursue a parallel opportunity from a financial security standpoint, be very discreet. Don't ask don't tell is the best strategy in such case. If there is no conflict of interest, legal or ethical boundary being crossed, most of your associates will not care what you do, if you are able to do justice to both initiatives. In the long run, you may have to choose one.

While you may be up front with your manager about this set up, it is never a good idea to discuss with your customers.

Recognizing Customers

Everyone likes to be recognized. That is an important need of every human being. Understand and act according to that psychology. Strive to make your customer contacts successful, get promoted and or recognized within their companies or departments.

Small and large vendors invite customers to events and recognize them in public. Collaborate with your marketing and events management team to engage with your customer contacts.

Email

Get into the habit of reading your composed email again before sending. Correct typos, grammar, and composition flow before sending. Start with a greeting.

All Microsoft Office documents should be converted into PDF format, unless explicitly requested by a customer before sending to them or alliance partners. Go through your customer's training related to company rules around intellectual property (IP), personally identifiable information (PII), and approved methods of transferring information. People new to the corporate world often get in trouble with assumptions about what they can share and how they can share it. Always be mindful of your company's policies and rules for sharing documents and files.

Tough negotiations, touchy conversations should be avoided via email. It is advisable to pick up the phone or make an appointment to meet when an email exchange starts getting out of control. Seemingly interminable email exchanges often can be resolved in a comparatively short direct conversation. If possible, with an in-person conversation, you can watch their body language as they hear your side of the argument.

APPENDICES: CUSTOMER SUCCESS TEMPLATES

VISUALS, CHECKLISTS, CALLOUTS, AND OTHER similar aids help retain key thoughts after reading a substantive publication. They help memorize and remember key points or to look up easily for quick reference much after the publication was last read. This chapter is designed to serve this purpose. If appropriate, you can cut images from this chapter to pin up in your cubicles or offices.

APPENDIX A: QUARTERLY BUSINESS REVIEW

Quarterly Business Review (QBR) Meeting Checklist

QBR checklist is suggested for consideration before any post adoption meeting is scheduled with customers. In summary, CSMs are requested to collect meaningful information from customer and vendor side systems and resources.

- Published an agenda ahead of time?
- Collected usage metrics from your own internal vendor systems?
- Asked to collect data from customer managed third party systems (CRM or ERP) as related to your implementations.
- Sent adoption and feedback surveys to customer coordinator and selected champion users as appropriate?

GOLDEN RULE

Ask but don't push.

The chances of you receiving all the information prior to the first QBR are less. It is usually best to prepare your QBR presentation and usage viewpoint based on available data and avoid delays due to missing or requested data.

ORPHAN HOLD
DO NOT SHIP

H1 – 000000000269

ISBN 9781941478974

CLIENT	Alternate Sourcing
STATION	TPP Receiving Station 03
HELD	2026 – 10 – 08 08:54

SHELF

If its order arrives, scan this label at a receiving station.

QBR Meeting Preparation

QBR to do list will help you prepare for the meeting after all available data is collected by CSM.

- Analyze collected data ahead of time
- Review previous action items, check status and prioritize
- Ensure there is progress from previous conversations and action items
- Collect, document and present applicable successes at other related customers
- Collect ideas to help customers get better returns from existing investments in your platform
- Explore business expansion opportunities via minimal additional investments from customer

KEY TAKEAWAY

If the investment on expansion opportunities makes sense to the customer, they will gladly invest

QBR Meeting Structure and Best Practices

QBR meeting agenda and post meeting activities outlined below will help you make your business case better and help with your customer retention objectives laid out in this book.

- Walk through usage, health, utilization and performance metrics derived from vendor and customer's third-party systems
- Discuss impact of these metrics on productivity gains, time savings, revenue boosts or mitigated risks
- Share your (vendor's) product roadmap, vision, and growth plans
- Share product implementation ideas and successes at customer peers
- Share best practices and suggest configuration, process or team (governance) changes to drive better utilization of sold product
- Prepare list of action items for vendor and customer
- Follow through and drive completion of action items
- Collect feedback from participants

APPENDIX B: ADOPTION CHALLENGES ROOT CAUSE CHECKLIST

As an independent auditor or customer success manager coming into the project post implementation, you may be required to investigate rollout issues. Always put yourself in the shoes of the user, customer project manager, executive or buyer, and then ask one or more of the following questions to yourself to help with the investigation.

1. Will you use the product given the current state of the solution?
2. Will you promote it at your own organization?
3. Are there productivity gains, efficiency, risk mitigation, revenue boost or hard cost reduction benefits that can be achieved through this solution?
4. Is the product and implementation setup convenient and usable?
5. Is the solution worth the operating expense?
6. Are there better alternatives that are cheaper, better, and can be obtained with minimal expense?

Answers to these questions will help you understand why the product deployment may not be successful. Depending on what you can remediate and the resulting customer side expense, your customer may help you stay in the account.

Vendor resources should always have these questions in mind as they pursue activities in the customer touchpoint phases outlined earlier in the book. To save costs all around, it is in fact better to ask above questions much before the implementation is even attempted by the vendor roles engaged to support vendor product and implementations:

- As product manager: when you work with engineers to build products
- As user experience manager: when you design product interfaces
- As implementation and solution manager: when you configure solutions for implementations

APPENDIX C:
CUSTOMER SUCCESS REPORT FORMAT

Customer success report is commonly used by CSM personnel to have periodic meetings with supervisors. It outlines the state of the customer accounts in their entirety or individually. The metrics outlined in Part I of this book are reflected as dashboards for each of the customer accounts. In addition, they highlight renewal revenue at risk, along with all supporting measures CSMs are taking to meet and exceed these revenue targets. CSM software solutions are best designed to automate generation of these reports. I have outlined a few of the data points per customer, I used to track and highlight for each of my accounts when I was handling a CSM role.

To support sorting and filtering, create groupings such as by revenue from customer (such as less than 1 Million, 1-5 Million) and company size (enterprise/medium/low). Deployment status options could be: Starting Implementation (Just signed contract), Under Implementation or Deployed. Risk status options could be: Failing Implementation, Feature Gaps, Customer Resource Constraint, Vendor Resource Constraint, Unusable Interface, Lack of Interest from Users, Withholding Payment, Competitive Solution

FINANCIAL

Annual business*

Company size

continued...

- Cross-sell / upsell opportunities
- Key performance metrics
- Risk status
- Deployment status

CONTRACTUAL

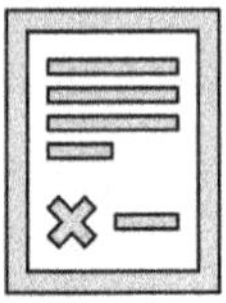

- Acquisition date
- Renewal date**
- QBR date***
- Account go live date
- Number of active users
- Number of licenses

OPERATIONAL

Last update / meeting date
Next meeting date
Meeting notes
Project plan link
Sponsor / contacts
Other customer personae
Customer success manager name
Other vendor personae
Scores (NPS, customer satisfaction)

**For SaaS annual licenses this information is readily available. If SAAS licensing not applicable consider historical annualized revenue over customer lifetime value.*
***Attempt to get all renewals to auto-mode with every renewal for two years.*
****Plan your QBRs ahead of renewal dates. Make sure you talk to each customer every few months.*

APPENDIX D: IMPLEMENTATION PROPOSAL TEMPLATES AND BEST PRACTICES

Sales customer touchpoint phase involves distribution of multiple proposals both for the product license and delivery of supporting implementation services. Most vendors have a good handle on the proposal format. I list below a high-level table of contents for the implementation services proposal to suggest full coverage.

- Cover letter
- Executive summary
- Implementation team setup
- High level flow diagram of implementation phases
- List of detailed steps with descriptions and expected milestones

continued...

Task ownership

List of implementation objectives

Work estimate and cost*

**For proposals, try to aggregate estimates across tasks as opposed to estimating effort for each task, unless explicitly requested by prospect.*

APPENDIX E: MEETING FORMATS AND BEST PRACTICES

This short cheat sheet will help CSMs help keep their meetings effective and efficient. Refer to the "Customer Meetings" chapter for the full list of considerations from a CSM standpoint.

- Strive to keep meetings short and to the point
- Share agenda ahead of time with summary of prior calls
- Check progress on action items socialized earlier
- Send request for action item updates ahead of meeting
- Take abundant notes and attempt to record all conversations
- Setup auto record option on web meetings

GLOSSARY

INDUSTRY TERMS COMMONLY USED IN corporate literature can be searched online for their meaning, using Internet search engines. Terms commonly used in this book are briefly defined here. In addition, I recommend looking up table of contents to locate the chapters covering other terms not specifically called out here. All team members and their roles involved from customer and vendor side are described in the People section in Chapter 2.

Collateral:
Collection of print, video, or audio media used to support the sale of a product or service or as used in the other customer touchpoint phases described in this book

Customer Experience:
Customers' perceptions—both conscious and subconscious—of their relationship with your brand resulting from all their interactions with your brand during the customer life cycle

Infographic:
A visual image that is used to represent information or data

Key Performance Indicator (KPI):
Value used to monitor and measure effectiveness

Net Promoter Score (NPS):
Score computed to understand and correct gaps in company's customer relationships

Nice to have:
A term used for projects that will have a marginal effect on company operations. Budget for such projects is limited and are typically assigned during surplus or extremely profitable years of the company

Persona (plural Personae):
A role assigned to the staff responsible for executing activities

Quarterly Business Review (QBR):
A Quarterly Business Review, or QBR, is a discussion meeting that you have with your customers on a quarterly basis

Sandbox:
A temporary and isolated environment to test, learn, implement or add features of an application, system or platform without affecting any production systems

Software as a Service (SAAS):
Software as a service (or SaaS) is a way of delivering applications over the Internet—as a service. Instead of installing and maintaining software, you simply access it via the Internet, freeing yourself from complex software and hardware management

Talk track:
Collection of pre-determined verbiage, identified and composed for delivery to external parties. This ensures consistent and authorized communication both written and verbal when interacting formally with others

Vendor:
Seller of the product and the employer of the resources serving the customer

REFERENCES

1. Net Promoter Score: Reichheld, Frederick F. (December 2003). "One Number You Need to Grow." *Harvard Business Review.*

2. Capability Maturity Model (CMM): CMM was developed and is promoted by the Software Engineering Institute (SEI), a research and development center sponsored by the U.S. Department of Defense (DoD). Paulk, Mark C.; Weber, Charles V; Curtis, Bill; Chrissis, Mary Beth (February 1993). "Capability Maturity Model for Software (Version 1.1)" (PDF). Technical Report. Pittsburgh, PA: Software Engineering Institute, Carnegie Mellon University. CMU/SEI-93-TR-024ESC-TR-93-177.

3. "Customer Experience Management: What it is and why it matters." SAS. Retrieved 2015-07-15. Customer experience is defined as your customers' perceptions—both conscious and subconscious—of their relationship with your brand resulting from all their interactions with your brand during the customer life cycle.

4. "What is Software as a Service (SaaS): A Beginner's Guide—Salesforce." Salesforce.com. Retrieved 2018-09-27.

ACKNOWLEDGMENTS

THIS BOOK IS BASED ON my experiences, observations, and interviews with accomplished customer success professionals. I thank all these fellow colleagues, supervisors, clients and partner consultants who directly and indirectly enlightened me with solid customer management principles over a two and half decade career. I wish these individuals, representing Fortune 500 companies in influential positions, continued success in their respective careers at financial institutions, industrial, management consulting companies, and other service industries.

I am grateful to several friends and family members in encouraging me to start the work, persevere with it, provide feedback and finally to finish it. My wife, Sapna, has been the source of my strength and energy throughout this and other professional endeavors. My mother and late grandfather has and will remain a source of inspiration and hope during trying situations. My kids', Krish's and Arush's, confidence in my abilities, has been contagious, encouraging me to continually refine the book till the very end. I thank my friends—Ann Jacob, Glance Fernandez, Shehzia Huq, Ramu Kallepalli and Jagathi Gururajan—for providing valuable ideas and updates.

Finally, this initiative wouldn't have been successful without the contributions of the publisher Windy City Publishers and its stellar team—Dawn McGarrahan Wiebe, Chris Nelson, Christy Phillippe, and Lise Marinelli. I thank Dawn for her operations coordination support, Chris for his attention to detail during the substantive editing, and Lise for taking on me as a client. I appreciate the collective team's patience and guidance throughout the book publishing process. I also thank the operations team—copy editing, typesetting, cover production, and proofing—diligently working in the background, for producing a quality publication that will serve the needs of customer success professionals for a long time!

ABOUT THE AUTHOR

PIYUSH AGRAWAL has led customer success, product implementation, product management, and product development functions at multiple software companies. He has spent more than a decade at a large management consulting firm, where customer relationships meant everything in business. He has audited and remediated findings of numerous software implementations at Fortune 100 organizations. Piyush has taken the customer relationship management ideas and practices outlined in this book and implemented them to create successful business and entrepreneurial initiatives with multimillion dollar returns over the years.

Piyush has captured in this book relevant customer success experiences from his long career with the goal of equipping those new to the workforce or looking for a career in the customer success field. To help vendors institutionalize the recommendations in this book, Piyush founded Latviv, a SaaS platform, aimed at helping Customer Success leaders. Latviv's goal is to maintain the spark in corporate relationships, during implementations, deployments and beyond.

Latviv is the combination of two root words "lat" and "viv." They stand for relationship and vitality—collectively standing for vitalizing relationships. Latviv offers a combination of content, services, and software to help vendors manage their customer relationships better. For representative thought leadership content, please check Latviv's Resources page (https://latviv.com/resources).

www.ingramcontent.com/pod-product-compliance
Lightning Source LLC
Chambersburg PA
CBHW061547250926
52052CB00010B/3097
9781941478974